MW00585357

Passport

To Your National Parks® Companion Guide

Southeast Region

Help Us Keep This Guide Up to Date

Every effort has been made by the author and editors to make this guide as accurate and useful as possible. However, many things can change after a guide is published—trails are rerouted, regulations change, techniques evolve, and so on.

We would love to hear from you concerning your experiences with this guide and how you feel it could be improved and kept up to date. While we may not be able to respond to all comments and suggestions, we'll take them to heart, and we'll also make certain to share them with the author. Please send your comments and suggestions to the following address:

FalconGuides
Reader Response/Editorial Department
P.O. Box 480
Guilford, CT 06437

Or you may e-mail us at:

editorial@GlobePequot.com

Thanks for your input, and happy trails!

Passport

To Your National Parks® Companion Guide

Southeast Region

Your Complete Guide to Cancellation Stamp Collecting

Randi Minetor

GUILFORD, CONNECTICUT
HELENA, MONTANA

AN IMPRINT OF THE GLOBE PEQUOT PRESS

To buy books in quantity for corporate use
or incentives, call **(800) 962–0973**
or e-mail **premiums@GlobePequot.com**.

FALCONGUIDES®

Text design by Nancy Freeborn
Maps by Tim Kissel © Morris Book Publishing, LLC

Library of Congress Cataloging-in-Publication Data is available on file.

ISBN: 978-0-7627-4473-2

Printed in the United States of America
10 9 8 7 6 5 4 3 2 1

Contents

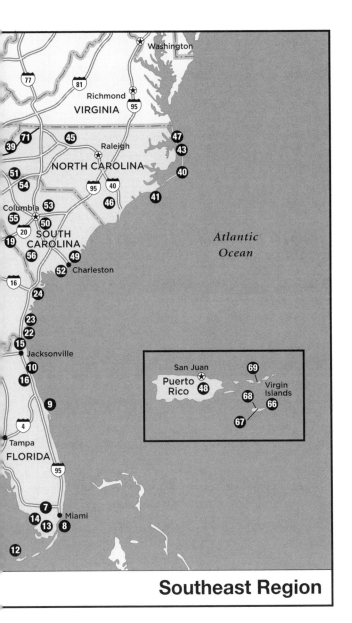

Southeast Region

National Trails that Cross Multiple States

About the Author

Preface

Friends and fellow Passport To Your National Parks® cancellation collectors have asked me why I took on the enormous project of creating a guidebook for my favorite hobby—an endeavor that has become a wonderful and endlessly fascinating part of my husband's and my life over the last seven years.

The need for this book hit me squarely between the eyes on a steamy August evening in 2002, when we stood in an empty Montana parking lot gazing at an inconspicuous green sign not 10 feet away that sealed our fate: PARK OPEN 8:30 A.M. TO 7:30 P.M. CENTRAL TIME.

Just across the state line in North Dakota stood the Fort Union Trading Post National Historic Site, our early evening destination, all rustic and inviting . . . and closed. Despite my calling ahead to check the closing time, despite the 90 miles of virtually empty road we'd traveled, and despite our fine planning . . . we had failed in our quest to collect our Passport cancellation.

Where had we gone wrong?

Nic and I had driven to North Dakota from our upstate New York home on an extended loop road trip that took the three of us—including June, my mother-in-law—to eleven official National Park sites across South and North Dakota, Montana, and Wyoming. For most people, such a trip through the scenic wonders of America's western prairie—the Badlands, the Black Hills, Wind and Jewel Caves, and the cataclysmic volcanic rupture that created Devils Tower—would be thrilling enough . . . but Nic and I traveled for a higher purpose. We were driven by our determination to collect Passport To Your National

Parks® cancellations at every park—and in some cases, to collect three, four, even five or more in one stop.

We'd hiked the rambling, wildflower-strewn quarry at Pipestone National Monument in Minnesota, descended more than 300 steps into the claustrophobic passageways of South Dakota's Wind Cave, and sat with thousands of spectators on benches in the late evening half-light to see Mount Rushmore's faces cast into shadows. We'd imagined Richard Dreyfuss's famed *Close Encounters of the Third Kind* mashed-potato sculpture of Devils Tower while standing at the base of its real-life counterpart, and we'd listened, enraptured, as a National Park Ranger revealed the irony in General Custer's ill-conceived battle at Little Bighorn. At every stop, we began our visit at the park bookstore, where we stamped our Passport book to commemorate the day. We came to get the cancellation, but we stayed because of the wonders we found.

Now in the home stretch, we had swooped down to the North Unit of Theodore Roosevelt National Park to get the Passport cancellation before the visitor center closed at 4:30 P.M., then made the drive back through the grasslands to Fort Union. On the way, I pulled out my mobile phone and called Fort Union to double-check the closing time. "Seven-thirty P.M.," the ranger confirmed. Not for one moment would it have occurred to me to respond with another question: "In which time zone?"

A funny thing happens to the time zone line in North Dakota. It zigzags along the edges of a dozen counties and through the middle of several, making the correct time a mystery to any unsuspecting traveler. Roughly following the path of the Missouri River, the time zone line even confuses some residents, who set their clocks to central time even though their neighborhoods are officially in mountain time.

So there was no way for us to know that in the top northwestern corner of the state, the time zone line veers sharply west, then follows the state border straight up to Canada.

We cruised up the long drive to the fort itself, enjoying the light of early evening as it turned the prairie the color of maple

syrup. Then all three of us gasped at once. A tiny sign read:
PARK OPEN 8:30 A.M. TO 7:30 P.M. CENTRAL TIME.

We looked at our watches. It was 6:45 P.M. mountain time . . . 7:45 P.M. central time.

Normal, sane travelers who had not been bitten by the Passport To Your National Parks® bug would have shrugged and driven away, skipping the fort altogether or leaving it for another vacation. We, however, schlepped back to Fort Union two days later to collect our cancellation, while Nic's mom sat in the back seat, counted yellow-headed blackbirds in the open fields, and chuckled at our misguided quest. The 97-mile back-track and hour-long visit to the fort—which turned out to be a charming fur-trading post with a droll mercenary perspective on the settlement of the Old West—set our trip back almost a full day.

On the return trip to Fort Union, Nic said casually, "If you're ever going to write another book, it should be a guide to the Passport program—so we never get stuck like this again."

This is that book.

The Passport program opens the door to magical moments and experiences you'll remember for a lifetime. With this book, you'll spend more time enjoying the parks and traveling to new places because you'll know exactly where to collect your Passport To Your National Parks® cancellations. I'm so pleased to have the opportunity to share this grand adventure with you and the hundreds of thousands of Passport cancellation collectors throughout the country. Enjoy your journey. Perhaps, on some distant mountain, in the recesses of a subterranean cavern, or in a visitor center in the nation's heartland, we'll meet and share our stories. I'll look forward to seeing all of your cancellations!

Acknowledgments

No project of this magnitude can come together unless many hands and minds join to make it happen—and I have literally hundreds of people to thank for their roles in bringing these field guides to bookshelves across America. In this limited space, I will acknowledge just a few of these helpful, encouraging, and supportive individuals.

First, I cannot say enough about the patient and persevering Scott Adams, executive acquisitions editor for The Globe Pequot Press, and my extraordinary agent, Regina Ryan, for supporting this project from the beginning and seeing it through many channels and challenges over many months to bring about its eventual birth. I am grateful to my copy editor, the amazing Tracy Salcedo-Chourré, and to Jan Cronan and Shelley Wolf at Globe Pequot for their efforts to streamline, simplify, and make this series the best it can be. Likewise, I thank Jason Scarpello and Chesley Moroz of Eastern National for their willingness to participate in this next extension of the Passport To Your National Parks® program. Rachel Shumsky; and later Eileen Cleary, at Eastern National maintained the list of Passport cancellation stamps at Eastern National's retail Web site, www.eparks.com, and they were quick to provide additional information when I needed it.

Many fellow Passport cancellation stamp collectors were generous with their time and knowledge as I tackled the daunting task of pinpointing locations for every known, documented, and active cancellation in the country. Nancy Bandley's amazing National Park Travelers Club Master List was a tremendous tool, and I thank her for the use of this excellent information source. I am particularly grateful to my Internet friend John D. Giorgis, whose encyclopedic knowledge of the national parks system and his own adventurous travel tales were of great help—I do hope that John succeeds in his dream of becoming Secretary of the Interior one day. Dan Elias, Charlie and Rett Davenport-Raspberry, Greg Parkes, and Coleen Tighe all offered information and assistance, and I can't thank them enough for their insights.

Hundreds of national park and national heritage area rangers, staff members, supervisors, and volunteers answered my questions and took the time to return my calls, find facts, track down old cancellations, and verify new ones for me, often providing new kernels of information about their sites and the activities and lessons available at each. My respect for the National Park Service grew with each passing day as I connected with these well informed, gracious, and helpful people across the country. I thank all of them for their guidance, assistance, comments, and recommendations about the Passport program, as well as for their unfailing cheerfulness. In particular, I am grateful to Phil Noblitt at the Blue Ridge Parkway and Gail Bishop at Gulf Islands National Seashore for their patience in answering my questions and collecting information for me. Andrea Sharon at the National Trails Office was especially helpful in tracking down facts and helping me find all of the cancellations for the Trail of Tears, including the placement of new cancellations for this trail in Alabama.

Here at home, I would be struggling through the final fact-checking to this day if not for my devoted and uncomplaining assistant, Dan O'Donnell, who followed up with every park and property and checked every cancellation's availability. To Martin Winer, my "writing date" buddy and lifelong friend, I am grateful for the long afternoons we passed with laptops and java in coffeehouses and sandwich shops throughout Rochester while each of us worked on our separate projects. There is nothing better than a friend who knows when to talk and when to just let be.

Finally, to my husband, Nic, the love of my life and the man who opened up this world of travel for me by sharing his passion for the two-lane blacktop, and then by discovering the Passport program and launching our own cancellation quest . . . may our travels be long, may the wind be at our backs, and may we never run out of open roads to drive, nor days in which to drive them.

Introduction

Passport Stampers, Start Your Engines!

So you've crisscrossed the United States by car, plane, train, and bus, you've traversed scenic rivers by powerboat, airboat, kayak, and canoe, you've hiked rolling foothills, climbed summits, and gazed down into massive canyons. You've stood at the top of Yosemite National Park's Sentinel Dome, trekked across the fire-hot sands of Death Valley, canoed the rushing Middle Delaware River, and camped among the alligators in the Everglades. You've visited every major Civil War battlefield and every president's mansion, and you've seen every bed in which George Washington once slept.

That's all great, but did you get the Passport cancellation?

The coveted Passport cancellation—the symbol of the Passport To Your National Parks® program—has moved from its humble beginning as a souvenir of happy National Park travelers to become a goal in itself. Today more than 1.3 million families own the little blue book that has developed into a national pastime, and more than 75,000 of these books sell in National Park bookstores every year.

If you're a Passport owner, you know what I know: Passport cancellation collecting is no casual matter. Chances are you've planned at least one vacation with the goal of visiting the most national park sites in a single day or week, stopping at each visitor center to stamp your Passport book with the 1¼-inch-wide, dated cancellation that proves you were there.

The Passport To Your National Parks® is a breast-pocket-sized book that contains instructions for its use, basic maps of each of its nine regions, and blank pages for the collection of rubber stamp cancellations and for sets of colorful, adhesive-backed stamps issued on an annual basis. Collectors will stop at Passport cancellation stations in whatever national park they visit and imprint their Passport books with the rubber stamp cancellation they find there. Each cancellation has an adjustable date, so it is a permanent reminder of the very day the Passport holder visited the park.

Cancellations record the date of your visit.

While the National Park Service currently divides the nation into seven geographic regions, the Passport program recognizes nine regional divisions to achieve an even distribution of parks over all of the service's geographic regions. Regions are designated in the Passport book by color, and each region includes a color-block map of included states, a list of the parks in that region, and blank pages for collection of *two* kinds of stamps: the *rubber stamp cancellations* showcased in this guide and *full-color, self-adhesive stamps* that are part of the Passport To Your National Parks® Annual Stamp Series.

The color-coding extends to the cancellations themselves: Cancellation stamps at each national park have ink colors that coincide with their regional divisions. In other words, a cancellation in Pennsylvania will have light blue ink to match the Mid-Atlantic Region's designated color in the Passport book, a Maine cancellation will have golden brown ink to match the North Atlantic Region's color, and so on.

It may also be interesting to note that some cancellations are expressed in a combination of upper case and lower case type; others are typeset in all capital letters.

A note on the Annual Stamp Series: The self-adhesive sets, issued every spring, include ten full-color stamps. One park from each of the nine regions is showcased on a separate stamp with a photograph and brief description; each set also includes a larger National Stamp honoring a park that's celebrating a special anniversary or milestone in that year. Like the cancellations, the self-adhesive stamps each have a color bar that matches the region's color, making them very easy to place on the correct pages in the Passport book. The stamp sets—including those issued in previous years—are readily available at the parks and on the Internet at www.eparks.com. *Because the stamp sets are so easy to obtain, they are not the focus of this Passport program companion guide. Instead, I focus on the cancellations, which must be secured at the various sites themselves.*

In 2006, the twentieth anniversary of the Passport program was recognized with the introduction of the Passport To Your National Parks® Explorer, a deluxe Passport package that provides more detailed maps, more stamping pages, a ring binder that allows users to insert and remove pages, a water-resistant, zipper-closed outer cover, pockets for maps, brochures, and personal items, a pen, and a handy carrying strap. The Passport To Your National Parks® companion guides are the right size to slip into the Explorer's inside pocket.

You may choose to chase every Passport cancellation in every park or affiliate, including the many duplicate cancellations scattered through far-flung visitor centers and other cancellation stations, or you may prefer to collect just one cancellation from each park as you happen across it. You also may want to collect "bonus cancellations," unofficial cancellations of every shape, size, color, and form, found in hundreds of national parks as well as in incalculable numbers of unrelated sites in every state (more on these below).

So successful is this program that there are now more than 1,500 cancellations available in 391 national parks and in dozens of National Park Service affiliates! This guide will tell you exactly where to find them, extending the pleasure of your travel experiences by taking you into areas you might never discover on your own. You'll see more of each park, you'll gain a better understanding of why the U.S. Department of the Interior preserves these natural, historic, and cultural places, and you'll come home with a sense of accomplishment and a burning desire to hit the road again as soon as possible...because there are more cancellations out there, more places to see, and more two-lane blacktop roads to conquer.

A (Very) Brief History of Passport To Your National Parks®

In 1986, the National Park Service entered into a joint agreement with Eastern National, the organization that owns and manages the bookstores in most of the national parks east of the Mississippi River. The idea was simple: Create a program that provides visitors to the national parks with a free memento and invites them to increase the frequency and quantity of their national park visits by encouraging them to collect Passport cancellations.

The Passport To Your National Parks® program began with just one cancellation at each park, but as it grew, so did the number of cancellations offered at many of the larger parks. Over the course of years, parks began to order additional cancellations. Participation in the program has always been voluntary, but no park has rejected the program (with the exception of Hohokam Pima National Monument in Arizona, which is not open to the public). In fact, hundreds of sites have chosen to expand the potential for Passport stamping within their boundaries. The smallest parks may have just one cancellation on the property, but the more expansive parks—Great Smoky Mountains, Yellowstone, Grand Canyon, Acadia, Olympic, Everglades, Delaware Water Gap, and many others—offer anywhere from five to seventeen cancellations in bookstores, visitor centers, museums, train depots, ranger stations, lighthouses, and information kiosks, luring collectors to stray from the main paths and discover the hidden treasures beyond.

This guide will help you find the cancellations that you want to collect, while bringing others to your attention that you might never find on your own. Collect the ones that interest you, ignore the rest, and enjoy the Passport program in the way that suits your lifestyle, your budget, and your enthusiasm.

Duplicate Versus Unique: Which Cancellations You'll Find in the Parks

As of this writing, more than 1,500 official Passport To Your National Parks® cancellations are documented throughout the 391 National Park Service sites, affiliated areas, and heritage corridors.

Many parks place duplicate cancellations at visitor centers and other sites throughout their units, providing easy access for collectors who may only make one stop within the park. For example, Acadia National Park in Maine offers a generic cancellation at every visitor center throughout the park, for a total of six duplicates.

Meanwhile, at the same park, there are twelve cancellations with location-specific text, providing collectors with unique cancellations for Blackwood Campground, Schoodic Peninsula, Isle au Haut, Seawall Campground, Islesford, Jordan Pond, and others.

A generic, duplicate cancellation and a unique place-specific cancellation.

Some Passport stampers collect all the duplicates as well as the unique cancellations they find in their travels. The idea of collecting an imprint from every Passport cancellation in the country appeals to some hard-core stampers, and they will return to parks again and again when new cancellations are added, even if they are identical to the originals.

Other collectors will skip the duplicates, collecting only the unique cancellations they find in each park. Each method provides its own rewards: Duplicate cancellation collecting will fill a Passport book quickly with places and dates, while collecting only the unique cancellations may save time on the road that would otherwise be spent chasing down duplicates.

In each park's entry, I note the unique cancellations and the duplicates to help you determine what you'd like to collect in the time you have. Cancellations that exist in only one location, with no duplicates, are noted in this guide as "unique" with a special $\mathbf{0}$ icon. These are the most precious cancellations to most Passport cancellation collectors, as each is available at only one place in the entire country. Knowing which cancellations are unique will help you plan your travels for maximum collecting. Those cancellations that can be collected in any number of locations are noted in this book as "duplicate" with a corresponding $\mathbf{0}$ icon.

Bonus Cancellations

In addition to the official cancellations, many Passport stampers collect the irregular "bonus" cancellation stamps they come across in their travels.

Bonus cancellations can come in any shape, size, or form. Some parks have a series of bonus cancellations in animal shapes, while others provide a commemorative cancellation to celebrate an important anniversary or milestone. Some are complex, depicting an entire landscape, scene, or architectural detail, while still others are simply larger and square instead of the regulation size and circular shape.

Travelers find these additional cancellations within and beyond the perimeters of the national parks: in the bookstores or offices of state-owned parks and historic sites, at presidential libraries, or at privately owned attractions. The rampant success of the Passport program certainly would encourage sites that are not part of this or any other stamping program to join in the fun.

A complete list of these odd and often transitory bonus cancellations would make this book too unwieldy to carry on stamping trips, but if you would like a list of all the bonus cancellations documented to date, visit www.parkstamps.org (the National Park Travelers Club Web site) and click on Master List.

About Changed and Missing Cancellations and Where to Send Updates

The Passport To Your National Parks® companion series endeavors to bring you the most accurate information possible about where to find Passport cancellation stamps in all National Park Service sites and affiliates.

Because the Passport program includes so many participating sites, changes can take place in the program without the knowledge of The Globe Pequot Press or this author. Cancellations sometimes wear out, become too damaged to use, are misplaced, or disappear entirely in the hands of selfish souvenir hounds. In addition, the increase in volunteers at national park sites, caused in part by recent budget constraints, means that many frontline information desk and visitor center assistants are not familiar with the Passport program.

Cancellations are often reordered, and staff members do not always order identical cancellations to those that have been lost or damaged. You are virtually certain to encounter occasional variations in spelling, punctuation, use of contractions, and actual wording on cancellations when compared to the cancellations listed in these guides. The original cancellation may be long gone or forgotten. You may hope that it is lingering in a desk drawer, waiting for an intrepid collector to inquire about it . . . but in reality, the chances of this are slim.

If you find that the cancellation you've collected at any site is not the one you expected, please contact me at foundstamp@minetor.com. I will make note of the change, post it on my official Web site at www.minetor.com/travel books, and pass the change on to the National Park Travelers Club for updating on the club's Master List. If you can e-mail a jpeg scan of your cancellation and include the exact location in which you found it, as well as your name, you will receive acknowledgement for your efforts on www.minetor.com/travelbooks.

Please do not harass rangers or any other park staff member or volunteer about missing cancellations. If you've inquired and the cancellation is not available, it's time to move on to your next stop, or to take some time to enjoy the park, visitor center, contact station, or historic site and its surroundings.

Needless to say, if you're traveling to a particularly out-of-the-way stamping location, call before you drive to be sure the cancellation is available.

Some Rules for Collecting Cancellations

The first and most important rule of Passport cancellation collecting is to enjoy the parks, whether you visit for an hour, a day, a week, or an entire season. We collect Passport cancellations because we love the parks in which they are found. Walk, bike, swim, paddle, explore, and learn as you travel.

Perhaps it's not necessary to say this, but Rule #2 is to show respect for the parks. The old adage, "Take nothing but pictures, leave nothing but footprints," holds true every day, and Passport stampers are leaders in demonstrating their commitment to park preservation. Leave artifacts or natural resources where you find them, pack out your own litter and that of others, and do no harm to the landscapes you came to admire.

About "Stamp and Run"

Here comes the collector, Passport book in hand, dashing to the cancellation station a few minutes before closing. He grabs the cancellation stamp, flips pages, bangs the stamp down onto the ink pad and smacks a quick imprint into his book...then rushes out again, with hardly a word of greeting to the staff member, ignoring the educational displays and the items for sale in the bookstore.

The dreaded "stamp and run" is the fastest way to meet the angry side of a park ranger—both because of the stamper's obvious disinterest in the park itself, and because the stamp-and-run perpetrator can appear indifferent, unfriendly, or down-right rude. Passport cancellation seekers take heed: The ranger who is frustrated by your apparent lack of interest could be the same ranger who will come to your aid when you've strayed off the trail in the forest, or help you limp back to the visitor center when you turn an ankle on a rocky path.

If you must stamp and run, stop for a moment to explain the reasons for your abrupt behavior to the ranger or staffer behind the desk. Ask the ranger what's new at the park, and listen to the options for ways to extend your visit or plan a return trip. We all encounter days when nothing goes as planned, and we arrive at a park just in time to stamp the Passport before the visitor center shuts down for the night. But there still may be a pleasant twilight walk, an unexplored path, a previously overlooked historic structure, or a turnout with a wondrous view that we did not know existed until we asked.

Talk to Passport Fans Online

Thanks to the Web, Passport cancellation collectors from all over the country can connect and talk to one another, sharing lists of cancellations, secrets for obtaining record numbers of cancellations in single trips, and much, much more.

One of the best resources you'll find online is the Master List, a gargantuan Microsoft Excel document updated on a biweekly basis by Nancy Bandley. Known as the "Stamp Queen," Nancy boarded a seaplane with her husband, Dennis, and reached her 388th park—Aniakchak National Monument and Preserve in Alaska—in June 2005. This list not only catalogs all of the official cancellations, it also lists every bonus, or unofficial, cancellation discovered to date, as well as the lost, retired, or stolen cancellations that are no longer available.

You can find the list on a Web discussion board run by the National Park Travelers Club at www.parkstamps.org, one of several sites at which Passport cancellation collectors share anecdotes and discoveries from the road.

If a motorcycle is your preferred vehicle, check out the Iron Butt Association's National Park Service Motorcycle Touring forum at http://forums.delphiforums.com/NPSTouring/ messages. These itinerant road warriors consider traveling from park to park an endurance sport. They know all the ins and outs of collecting, and their tips for safe, long-distance riding are invaluable to any cycle enthusiast.

How to Use This Book

This companion guide series is divided into nine books to match the regions in the Passport program. The states are listed alphabetically within each region, and the parks are alphabetized within each state.

In addition to the 391 official national parks, you'll find national park affiliated areas and National Heritage Areas and Corridors listed within each state. Virtually all of these affiliates have Passport cancellations, although participation in the Passport program is spottier because the sites are less centralized. Management of affiliated areas and National Heritage Areas and Corridors is in the hands of state and local agencies rather than the National Park Service. Some are exquisitely managed and maintained—the Oklahoma City National Memorial is a standout in this regard—while others are spread out across a wide geographic area, making it more difficult for management to keep tabs on the location and maintenance of Passport cancellations.

Here's what you'll find on each page of this guide:

- The official National Park Service name and designation for the park.

- The state and town or city in which the park is located (or where the park's headquarters is located for multilocation parks).

- The park's main information telephone number and Web address—you'll need these to double check park hours, to make certain that the park is actually open on the day you want to go there, and to plan the activities you'd like to enjoy during your visit. Even though park hours are provided in this book, anything from bad weather to budget shortages can close a visitor center or outlying building without notice.

- The park's time zone.
- Total number of cancellations at each park, with additional totals for any cancellations for other parks at the site.
- The degree of difficulty in obtaining the park's Passport cancellations. Every park has a rating of **Easy, Tricky, Challenging,** or **Heroic,** helping you understand the hurdles you must vault to collect all of the cancellations in each park.

Easy: The park is open 362 days or more each year and has only one or two cancellations, which are readily accessible at the bookstore or visitor center. Essentially, if you show up during business hours any day but Thanksgiving, Christmas, or New Year's Day, the cancellation is yours.

Tricky: Something's up at this park, and you'll need to be alert to get the cancellation. The park is open only during limited hours or on an erratic or seasonal schedule. There's more than one cancellation, and there's an obstacle—the cancellation stamp is hidden in a desk drawer, a long-closed visitor center waiting for repairs, a task that must be performed before the cancellation can be obtained. Look for the "Stamping tips" to find out what's going on.

Challenging: There are lots of cancellations in this park, and it may take more than one day to get them all and still enjoy what this park has to offer. Cancellation collecting may require an unusual physical effort, like a long walk (more than a mile) to the stamping site, or the many units involved are open on a limited basis. You'll go well out of your way to finish stamping in this park. The "Stamping tips" will help you figure out what to do—and for the parks with the most cancellations, there's a suggested route for maximum stamping success.

Heroic: Slap on that seasickness patch and strap in! You'll need to endure a long ferry ride—or two—on choppy water, charter a seaplane, or jet out to an exotic island to get this one. There may be only one cancellation at each of these parks, but it will be hard-won, and you'll be talking about this trip for years to come.

- A short description of the park and why it exists, providing baseline information about what you can see, do, or learn when you go.

- "Stamping tips," with cautions, twists, and turns encountered by some of the most well traveled Passport participants in the country.

- "Don't miss this!" takes you beyond the brochure to find the gems in each park—sights, sounds, and activities you might not discover on your own. "Don't miss this!" is highlighted with an ❶ icon.

- Park hours and fees are broken down by individual visitor center or other cancellation stamp location.

- Driving directions to the sites from the nearest major highways or cities.

- Stamping locations and what the cancellations say is the meat-and-potatoes for each park. The cancellation's specific location, any pertinent information on that location, and the cancellation's exact text are provided in this section. The text on each cancellation is listed uniformly to help you determine if you have found the correct cancellation. The text that arches around the top half of the cancellation is listed first. A "/" (forward slash) signals the end of the top text, and the text following the "/" fills the bottom half of the cancellation. *The text is listed exactly as it appears on the cancellation: If it's listed in this guide in all capital letters, then the cancellation itself was made that way. Occasionally a misspelling appears on a cancellation; these are not corrected in this guide, but presented as they appear.*

Unique cancellations are identified with a ❶. These cancellations have no duplicates. There's only one place to find each of these, so you'll want to build stops for these cancellations into your travel plans.

Duplicated cancellations are identified with a ❶. These cancellations can be found in more than one place.

While we believe that all the existing cancellations have been cataloged here, you may come across new or hitherto undetected official Passport cancellation stamps that are not in this book. If so, we want to hear from you! Please send any updates to me at foundstamp@minetor.com. Include the text of the cancellation, the place you found it, and as much detail as possible about where this cancellation resides. If possible, send a jpeg scan of the cancellation. I'll post updates at my Web site for this purpose, www.minetor.com/travelbooks.

In addition to this book and your official Passport, you need one more thing: America the Beautiful—The National Parks and Federal Recreational Lands Pass. This pass will provide you and the other passengers in your single-family vehicle (or your spouse, parents, and children) with free or discounted admission for one year to every park site in the system, as well as other sites managed by the federal government. You'll find that your pass will pay for itself in one trip. Purchase your pass from the National Parks Foundation at www.nationalparks.org, or at any national park site.

Buckle up—it's time to hit the road.

The Southeast Region

Many of the nation's greatest triumphs and tragedies took place in the states south of Virginia and east of the Mississippi River, and as a result, the Southeast Region contains more than half of all national battlefields and battlefield parks protected by the National Park Service. Not only will you find capsules of Civil War history spread throughout these states—within the remains of coastal and inland forts, on farmer's fields turned battlegrounds, and in historic homes and government sites— you'll also discover Revolutionary War sites that produced important wins for the patriots and sealed America's future. The lower three of the original thirteen colonies, the disputed lands along Florida's coastline, and the new frontier glimpsed beyond Cumberland Gap and over the Blue Ridge Mountains combine in this region to show us an America in development, a new land with new ideas, new challenges, and new solutions.

Just as you will see military victories and defeats in these states, you'll also see sites that commemorate some of the nation's most troubling decisions and the atrocities that followed them. The Southeast Region introduces us to the Trail of Tears, the route along which U.S. Army regiments, empowered by an order signed into law by President Andrew Jackson, forced Native Americans from their homes and relocated them in reservations in the Oklahoma Territory. In Alabama, we learn of the march of hundreds of African Americans from Selma to Montgomery to protest state laws that forbid them from voting in elections, even though the federal government had granted them that right many decades before. The Georgia home of civil rights leader Dr. Martin Luther King Jr., the campus of Tuskegee Institute, and the historic site honoring the Tuskegee Airmen all remind us of times many remember firsthand, when

African Americans fought for basic human rights and won through peaceful demonstrations, non-violent resistance, and the bravery of ordinary individuals who did extraordinary things.

While all of the National Park Service official sites have Passport cancellations in this region, the **Mississippi Gulf Coast National Heritage Area** has no cancellations of its own. Part of this heritage area includes Gulf Islands National Seashore. There are cancellations for the seashore (covered in the Mississippi and Florida chapters of this guide), despite the 2004 and 2005 hurricanes that battered this Gulf of Mexico coastline, but no cancellations have been ordered to date that mention the heritage area itself.

Just before this guide went to press, the Underground Railroad Network to Freedom added cancellations in this region. While a dedicated entry on the Network to Freedom is not provided in this guide, its cancellations are listed at sites throughout the book.

Amtrak Trails & Rails Partnership Program

A special Passport cancellation stamp opportunity
www.nps.gov/trails&rails

Since the earliest days of the National Park Service, visits to the most remote and rugged parks often were accomplished by train—and it's this long association between national parks and train travel that led Amtrak and the National Park Service to create Trails & Rails, an unusual partnership that combines travel on the tracks with an opportunity to learn the natural and human history of the parks you pass along the way.

Here's how it works: When you buy a ticket on one of the participating trains and ride the train on one of the days the program is offered, you can take part in a lecture and question-and-answer session in the lounge car as you ride from one end of the train's route to the other. Led by well-versed volunteers, these programs provide in-depth information about one or more parks on the route . . . and at each program, Passport cancellation collectors can get a special cancellation that's only offered during these Trails & Rails sessions.

It sounds simple enough to acquire these cancellations, but it's trickier than you think. Most of the Trails & Rails programs are offered from Memorial Day to Labor Day, and only on certain days of the week—and if a volunteer turns out not to be available, the program may be scuttled for that trip. The cancellations are kept in a traveling trunk that the volunteer picks up before boarding, so they don't actually "live" on the trains, and are not available on days when there is no Trails & Rails program.

Additionally, you need to ride the trains from a specific departure point and to a specific disembarkation point to be sure that a Trails & Rails program is scheduled on that train. For example, the Sunset Limited train runs from Orlando, Florida, to Los Angeles, California, but the two Trails & Rails programs offered on this train take place between Del Rio and Alpine, Texas (for Amistad National Recreation Area), and between New Orleans, Louisiana, and Houston, Texas (for Jean Lafitte National Historical Park & Preserve). You need to be on the train between these cities to have access to the cancellations, as the volunteer guides board in the first city and depart in the latter.

In the off-season, from Labor Day until Memorial Day, these train-specific cancellations may be kept at the participating parks, but it's also possible they will languish in the traveling trunk until the next Memorial Day. If you are determined to collect these cancellations, the sure-fire way to do so is to ride the trains on the right days.

You can research all of the opportunities and buy your tickets on the Amtrak Web site at www.amtrak.com.

- First, choose your route by clicking on "Routes" and choosing the name of the train from the pull-down menu.

- When the information about your train comes up, scroll to the bottom of the page for the "At A Glance" listing.

- Click on the name of the train. A pdf file of the train's current schedule will download to your computer.

- Open the pdf file and scan the document for the Trails & Rails listing, probably at the bottom of the last page, where "Services" are listed. This will tell you the days on which the Trails & Rails program is offered on this route.

- Make your reservations online by clicking on the "Reservations" tab at the top of the page, or call (800) USA–RAIL to talk with a reservations specialist, who can confirm that the Trails & Rails program will be offered on your travel date.

    More information on the trains, participating parks, and routes is available at www.nps.gov/trails&rails.

Trails and Rails: Southeast Region

One train in the Southeast Region offers an Amtrak Trails & Rails cancellation.

The Crescent

Runs between Atlanta, Georgia, and New Orleans, Louisiana

☐ Martin Luther King Jr NHS/The Crescent Ⓤ

Alabama

1 Horseshoe Bend National Military Park

Daviston, Alabama
(256) 234–7111
www.nps.gov/hobe
Central time zone

Number of cancellations: One

Difficulty: Easy

About this site: Andrew Jackson, who would become the seventh president of the United States, distinguished himself as general of 3,300 men—including U.S. Army troops, Tennessee militia, and Cherokee and Lower Creek Indian allies—by winning a battle at the bend of the Tallapoosa River. The opposing force consisted of more than 1,000 Upper Creek (Red Stick) Indians defending their homeland from this invading army. The victory ended the Creek War, and the resulting peace treaty ceded twenty million acres of Alabama and Georgia—more than half the tribe's ancestral land—to the United States. Sixteen years later, President Jackson would sign the Indian Removal Bill, which ultimately led to the forced removal of all southeastern tribes living east of the Mississippi to the Indian Territory, now the state of Oklahoma.

Don't miss this! There are two ways to explore the battlefield: the auto loop and the Nature/Battlefield Hiking Trail, a 2.8-mile trail that traces the river bend and passes through several key points on the battleground: Cotton Patch Overlook, the Tohopeka Indian village, Gun Hill, and the site of the Red Stick barricade. It takes an hour or two to walk the entire trail, and you'll encounter some steep hills and low patches, but the trail gives you a sense of the land as it might have been in the days of battle, filled with pine and hardwood forests and babbling streams.

Hours: The visitor center is open daily year-round, from 9:00 A.M. to 4:30 P.M. The tour road is open from 8:00 A.M. to 5:00 P.M. The site is closed Thanksgiving, Christmas, and New Year's Day.

Fees: Admission to this park is free.

How to get there: The park is located on Alabama 49, 12 miles north of the town of Dadeville, between Dadeville and New Site. You can reach the site from U.S. Highway 280 and Alabama 22. Signs along both highways direct you to the site.

Stamping Locations and What the Cancellations Say

Horseshoe Bend Visitor Center

☐ Horseshoe Bend Nat'l Military Park/Tallaposa County, AL **❶**

2 Little River Canyon National Preserve

Fort Payne, Alabama
(256) 845–9605
www.nps.gov/liri
Central time zone

Number of cancellations: Five for the preserve, plus two cancellations for the Trail of Tears National Historic Trail and a cancellation for Russell Cave National Monument

Difficulty: Tricky

About this site: Flowing along the top of Lookout Mountain on a plateau formed by an erosion-resistant layer of sandstone, the Little River plunges down into Weiss Lake with such force that its impact has chiseled one of the longest and deepest canyons in the eastern states. Shale and sandstone walls drop steeply for 500 to 600 feet into the churning river below, where natural debris and impressive rapids are telltale signs of the river's power and strength.

Stamping tips: If you travel between May and August, you should be able to secure the cancellation at the Canyon Mouth Park entrance booth when a ranger is on duty. The booth has an unpublished telephone number, so calling ahead is not possible. The cancellation at the booth is a duplicate, so you'll only need to make this special effort if you're collecting every existing cancellation.

The cancellation at DeSoto State Park Lodge is that rarest of Passport stampers' quarries: It is available not only year-round, but around the clock. It's a duplicate of the cancellation at Russell Cave, however, so if you're pressed for time and planning a stop at the cave to pick up its cancellation as well, you may wish to skip DeSoto.

Park staff members warn that County Road 275 to the Canyon Mouth entrance booth is very steep, and it's not recommended for motorcycles. The park offers these directions for a shortcut to Canyon Mouth: Coming from the east on Alabama 35 (before you get to the preserve), you will see a grocery store on your right at an intersection. Turn left onto Alabama 273, follow it for 9 or 10 miles, and turn right at the sign for Canyon Mouth Park.

Don't miss this! Rock climbing, kayaking, swimming, rugged hiking, hunting, and fishing in season are favorite pastimes in this Southern Appalachian preserve. Whitewater paddling is recommended only for experts, as rapids can reach a treacherous Class VI, but the calmer pools lend themselves to a cool dip on a hot day. The challenging trails offer mountain bikers and horseback riders an exciting day's ride.

If all of these thrilling athletic experiences do not attract your interest, the scenery absolutely will, and the eight overlooks along Alabama 176 satisfy travelers with their panoramic views of Little River Falls and the surrounding canyon, created by thousands of years of river water rushing down from Lookout Mountain.

Hours: The park is open from dawn to dusk year-round.

The superintendent's office is open Monday to Friday from 8:00 A.M. to 4:30 P.M., and Saturday from 10:00 A.M. to 2:00 P.M. It is closed on all major holidays.

The Canyon Mouth Day Use Area entrance booth is open year-round from 8:00 A.M. to 7:00 P.M. Hours may be extended when daylight lasts longer, and hours may vary with seasons and weather.

DeSoto State Park Lodge is open twenty-four hours a day, seven days a week, year-round.

Gilbert H. Grosvenor Visitor Center at Russell Cave National Monument is open year-round from 8:00 A.M. to 4:30 P.M. It is closed Thanksgiving, Christmas, and New Year's Day.

Fees: A $3.00 per car day-use fee is charged at the Canyon Mouth Day Use Area. Otherwise, admission to this park is free.

How to get there: From Atlanta, Georgia, take Interstate 75 north to exit 290. Turn left after exiting onto Georgia 20. Follow the road 4 miles. Turn left onto U.S. Highway 411. Bear right onto Joe Frank Harris Parkway Southeast, and continue for 3 miles. Take the ramp onto US 411 south to Rome, Georgia. Take the U.S. Highway 27 north ramp, and continue on this road for 3 miles. Pick up GA 20 going west, and stay on GA 20 as it turns into Alabama 9. Follow AL 9 for 6 or 7 miles to its intersection with AL 35 toward Fort Payne. Turn right (north) on AL 35. Follow AL 35 for 16 to 20 miles to Little River Canyon National Preserve. Little River Falls will be on the left immediately before the bridge.

Stamping Locations and What the Cancellations Say
Superintendent's Office
2141 Gault Avenue North, Fort Payne
(256) 845–9605
To reach the office from the falls, cross the bridge on AL 35 and continue straight down the mountain for 5 miles to a flashing yellow light. At the light, bear right on a sharp curve. Go to the second light and turn right onto Alabama 11/Gault Avenue. Continue 17 blocks to the headquarters building.

☐ Little River Canyon National Preserve/Ft Payne, AL Ⓓ
☐ Trail of Tears NHT/Alabama Ⓓ

Canyon Mouth Day Use Ticket Booth
From the falls, turn right out of the driveway. Turn right again, onto Alabama 273, immediately beyond the bridge. Take this scenic drive about 10 miles to CR 275, turn right, and follow signs to the park.

☐ Little River Canyon National Preserve/Ft Payne, AL Ⓓ

DeSoto State Park Lodge
265 County Road 951, Fort Payne
(800) 568–8840 or (256) 845–5380
Follow AL 35 until you come to a flashing yellow light. Turn right onto DeSoto Parkway (CR 89) and follow the signs to the park. The cancellation is at the front desk.

□ Little River Canyon Nat'l Preserve/Fort Payne, AL Ⓓ

DeKalb County Tourist Association

1503 Glenn Boulevard Southwest
Fort Payne, Alabama
(888) 805–4740 or (256) 845–3957
From Interstate 59, take exit 218. Follow the access road to AL
35; go west on AL 35 (Glenn Boulevard). Continue to the tourist
association.

□ Little River Canyon National Preserve/Fort Payne, AL Ⓓ

Gilbert H. Grosvenor Visitor Center

Russell Cave National Monument
3729 County Road 98, Bridgeport
(256) 495–2672
From U.S. Highway 72, turn left onto County Road 75 west.
Go 1 mile to CR 98, turn right, and follow CR 98 north 4 miles to
the park entrance.

□ Little River Canyon Nat'l Preserve/Fort Payne, AL Ⓓ
□ Russell Cave National Monument/Bridgeport, AL 35740 Ⓤ
□ Trail of Tears NHT/Alabama Ⓓ

❸ Russell Cave National Monument

Bridgeport, Alabama
(256) 495–2672
www.nps.gov/ruca
Central time zone

Number of cancellations: One unique, plus one for Little River
Canyon National Preserve and one for the Trail of Tears National
Historic Trail

Difficulty: Easy

About this site: Long before the Europeans came to this part
of the continent, prehistoric tribes inhabited these hills and relied
on the natural resources around them for food, clothing, and
protection. One of these resources was the place we now call
Russell Cave, a naturally formed shelter that served as housing

more than 9,000 years ago—and now provides one of the most extensive and informative archaeological sites in the southeastern United States. Artifacts found in the cave fill the visitor center's displays with pottery, weapons, tools, and jewelry that provide hints about the lives of the first people to dwell in this corner of Alabama.

❶ Don't miss this! Take a guided tour to the prehistoric shelter, and watch staff members demonstrate skills that were critical to survival in millennia long past, such as making spear points, throwing a spear using an atlatl, and making fire with a bow drill.

For a nice, challenging walk, take the outdoor hiking path along Montague Mountain, or spend your time learning about the prehistoric people who lived within the cave walls by absorbing their story in the visitor center.

Hours: The cave is open daily year-round, from 8:00 A.M. to 4:30 P.M. It is closed Thanksgiving, Christmas, and New Year's Day.

Fees: Admission to this park is free.

How to get there: From U.S. Highway 72, follow County Road 75 north 1 mile to County Road 98. Follow CR 98 north 4 miles to the park entrance at 3729 CR 98.

Stamping Locations and What the Cancellations Say
Gilbert H. Grosvenor Visitor Center

☐ Russell Cave National Monument/Bridgeport, AL 35740 **❶**
☐ Little River Canyon Nat'l Preserve/Fort Payne, AL **❶**
☐ Trail of Tears NHT/Alabama **❶**

■4 Selma to Montgomery National Historic Trail

Hayneville, Alabama
(334) 877-1983
www.nps.gov/semo
Central time zone

Number of cancellations: One

Difficulty: Easy

About this site: While the Fifteenth Amendment of the Constitution—passed in 1870—granted every male American citizen the right to vote regardless of race, states with large populations of newly freed African-American slaves quickly found ways to work around the amendment, preventing these former slaves from registering to vote through poll taxes, literacy tests, and other prohibitive activities. Such discriminatory practices continued for nearly one hundred years with no consequences for the perpetrators. When civil rights activists and African-American citizens came together in Selma, Alabama, in March 1965 to take a public stand against this prejudice, they organized a series of marches that raised the issue to a new, higher level of visibility.

Five hundred peaceful demonstrators marched across the Edmund Pettus Bridge on March 7 on their way to the state capitol, only to be greeted on the other side by Alabama state troopers who met their non-violence with an aggressive, needlessly bloody attack that shocked and horrified the nation. Two weeks later, thousands of grimly determined marchers, undaunted by spring rains, chilly temperatures, and fear of further attacks, walked from Selma to Montgomery. The five-day, four-night, 54-mile march was observed on the nightly news in every living room in the country. Five months later, President Lyndon Johnson rewarded their courage by signing into law the Voting Rights Act of 1965, guaranteeing every African-American citizen the right to vote and thwarting individual states' attempts to undermine the law.

Don't miss this! A visitor center for this trail opened in Lowndes County in August 2006, one of three planned to interpret this trail's historic significance for tourists. Stops along the Selma to Montgomery National Historic Trail tell the story of the five-day civil rights march and the support it received from selected members of the communities involved. Stops that stand out along the route include the Brown Chapel AME Church in Selma and the bridge where Dr. Martin Luther King Jr. and hundreds of marchers crossed on March 25, 1965. The four campsites where marchers spent nights are marked along the U.S. Highway 80 route. The fourth campsite, at the City of Saint Jude Historic District in Montgomery, is where Dr. King and 2,000 marchers received shelter on the night before the march's final push to the state capitol.

Hours: The trail is open twenty-four hours a day, seven days a week, year-round.

The Lowndes County Interpretive Center is open daily year-round, from 9:00 A.M. to 4:30 P.M. It is closed Thanksgiving, Christmas, and New Year's Day.

Fees: Admission to this park is free.

How to get there: From Birmingham, follow Interstate 65 south, and take exit 212 to Clanton. Take Alabama 145 south to Alabama 22, then follow AL 22 south to Selma. Take US 80 east to Montgomery.

From Atlanta, Georgia, take Interstate 85 south to Montgomery. Merge onto I–65 south, and exit onto US 80 westbound (exit 167). Follow US 80 for 43 miles to Selma.

The start of the trail is at Brown Chapel, AME Church in Selma, at 410 Martin Luther King Jr. Street. Follow the trail markers to scenic US 80 through Lowndes County. Continue on US 80 to Montgomery, ending at the Alabama State Capitol in Montgomery at 600 Dexter Avenue.

Stamping Locations and What the Cancellations Say

Lowndes County Interpretive Center
7002 US 80 West, Hayneville (White Hall)
(334) 877–1983 or (334) 877–1984
Located on US 80 midway between Selma and Montgomery
☐ Selma to Montgomery NHT/Lowndes County, AL ➊

5 Tuskegee Airmen National Historic Site

Tuskegee, Alabama
(334) 724–0922
www.nps.gov/tuai
Central time zone

Number of cancellations: One

Difficulty: Easy

About this site: The U.S. armed forces dubbed it a "military experiment"—the decision to train African-American men to become pilots in World War II, answering the demand to allow black servicemen to hold positions of responsibility as the war effort escalated. The small but prestigious Tuskegee Institute became the logical place to center this training program, and from 1942 to 1946, Tuskegee turned out nearly 1,000 pilots who were ready to serve their country and distinguish themselves in battle, as well as navigators, bombardiers, instructors, maintenance specialists, and many more—upward of 15,000 people who shared the title of Tuskegee Airmen. Together they flew more than 15,500 missions, shot down 260 enemy aircraft, and even sank an enemy destroyer, earning medals and honors including a Distinguished Unit Citation for "outstanding performance and extraordinary heroism."

Don't miss this! A new museum is expected to open in October 2008. Until then, enjoy one or more of the five videos about the airmen's history in the thirty-seat auditorium in the temporary visitor center, and then take a leisurely walk to the overlook at Moton Field, where the airmen received their primary flight training.

Hours: The site is open daily from 9:00 A.M. to 4:30 P.M. Closed Thanksgiving, Christmas, and New Year's Day.

Fees: Admission to this park is free.

How to get there: From Atlanta, Georgia, take Interstate 85 south toward Montgomery. Travel 150 miles south of Atlanta to exit 38, and turn left, going under the overpass. Travel 1 mile and turn left on Chappie James Avenue. Travel 0.5 mile to the visitor parking area on the left.

From Montgomery, take I–85 north toward Atlanta. Travel 40 miles to exit 38; turn right. Go 1 mile to Chappie James Avenue. Turn left and go 0.5 mile to the parking lot. The visitor center is at 1616 Chappie James Avenue.

Stamping Locations and What the Cancellations Say
Visitor center at Moton Field

☐ Tuskegee Airmen Nat'l Hist Site/Tuskegee, AL ➊

6 Tuskegee Institute National Historic Site

Tuskegee, Alabama
(334) 727–3200
www.nps.gov/tuin
Central time zone

Number of cancellations: One

Difficulty: Easy

About this site: Education—not simply learning to read and write, but also training to work in a profession—would prove to be the stepping-stone to independence and self-reliance for thousands of African Americans after the Civil War. Nowhere was this change in African-American life more apparent than at Tuskegee Normal School, a teaching college led by young principal Booker T. Washington, a former slave, and cofounded by Lewis Adams, a tradesman who had also risen from slavery, and George Campbell, a former slave owner.

Offering its first class in 1881, the school grew rapidly under Washington's leadership, adding faculty members including renowned scientist George Washington Carver and Robert Taylor, the first African-American architect to graduate from MIT. Today, Tuskegee University has more than 75 buildings and 5,000 acres, and is the only American college designated a National Historic District.

Don't miss this! One of the wonderful synergies of national-park-site touring is the opportunity to see the humble beginnings of some of the nation's greatest leaders, and then see the heights to which they rose later in life. That's why no tour of Tuskegee would be complete without visiting The Oaks, Booker T. Washington's tasteful, comfortable home on the institute's campus—especially if you have been to Virginia and seen the replica of Washington's childhood home, a slave's shack on a small plantation.

This redbrick, Queen Anne–style house was completed in 1900 for Washington and his family, and it stood out in Macon County for its forward-thinking modernity—fitted with steam heat, indoor plumbing, and electricity, the first to have such luxuries in the area.

Hours: The site is open daily year-round, from 9:00 A.M. to 4:30 P.M. It is closed Thanksgiving, Christmas, and New Year's Day. The Washington home is slated to reopen in late 2008 after renovations are completed.

Fees: Admission to this park is free.

How to get there: Take Interstate 85 north from Montgomery or south from Atlanta to exit 32. Exit right onto Pleasant Springs Drive. Travel 4 to 5 miles, following Tuskegee University signs, to Franklin Road. Turn left on Franklin Road, and go 4 miles to the traffic light. Turn left onto West Montgomery Road, then left again at the first traffic light into the Tuskegee University campus. The Kellogg Executive Conference Center is on the right, and the George Washington Carver Museum is directly behind and right of the Kellogg center. Parking is in the rear of the Kellogg center in the parking garage.

Stamping Locations and What the Cancellations Say

George Washington Carver Museum
Tuskegee University
(334) 727–3200

☐ Tuskegee Institute NHS/Tuskegee Institute, AL **ⓤ**

Florida

7 Big Cypress National Preserve

Ochopee, Florida
(239) 695–1201
www.nps.gov/bicy
Eastern time zone

Number of cancellations: Two

Difficulty: Easy

About this site: One of the last great wilderness areas in the state of Florida, this remarkable blend of temperate and tropical ecosystems provides visitors with opportunities to view species typical of both climates—alligators and tree snails side by side with white-tailed deer, bears, and the elusive Florida panther. Hardwood forests stand alongside mangrove swamps and cypress strands, and prairies give way to palm trees and orchids. The result is a wildlife and botanical viewing experience that cannot be found anywhere else in the country.

Stamping tips: It's easy to get the Ochopee cancellation. In years past the Florida National Scenic Trail cancellation has been kept in a drawer and offered only when collectors asked for it. If you don't see the cancellation on the desk, ask the ranger for it.

More than 40 miles of the Florida National Scenic Trail pass through the Big Cypress National Preserve, but don't be daunted by this fact, because in the rainy season (summer and fall), most of the trail is underwater. Don't assume this is wading territory! The water can quickly rise to your waist.

🛑 **Don't miss this!** Because of the unusual blending of climate zones in this preserve, the birding at Big Cypress can be truly breathtaking during the winter dry season. The endangered wood stork and the snail kite make their home here, as well as the red-cockaded woodpecker, a species on the verge of extinction. Drive the Loop Road (from Monroe Station off of U.S. Highway 41 back to US 41 at its junction with County Road 94), and you're sure to see common tropical birds and some of the rarities. To see the woodpecker, you'll need to hike into the pine woods very early in the morning. Ask a ranger at the Big Cypress Visitor Center at Oasis for this year's woodpecker nesting locations.

Hours: The preserve is open daily year-round, from 9:00 A.M. to 4:30 P.M. It is closed Christmas.

Fees: Admission to this park is free.

How to get there: Interstate 75, Florida 29, and US 41 all travel through the preserve. The Big Cypress Visitor Center is on US 41 at 33100 Tamiami Trail East.

Stamping Locations and What the Cancellations Say

Big Cypress Visitor Center at Oasis

☐ Big Cypress National Preserve/Ochopee, FL **Ⓤ**

☐ Big Cypress/Fla NS Trail **Ⓤ**

8 Biscayne National Park

Homestead, Florida
(305) 230–7275
www.nps.gov/bisc
Eastern time zone

Number of cancellations: One

Difficulty: Easy

About this site: At first glance, you won't see what makes Biscayne National Park an important area to protect and preserve, because 95 percent of this park is covered by water. Stand on the shore and turn around slowly, however, and you'll see the longest stretch of mangrove forest in eastern Florida; crystal clean Biscayne Bay, a virtually unsullied body of water that provides a home to hundreds of fish, bird, amphibian, and plant species; the northern islands of the Florida Keys, preserved as all of the Keys were before bridges and residential development took over; and the coral reef, the third largest of its kind in the world.

❶ Don't miss this! You can enjoy the park from the veranda at the visitor center, sitting in a comfy rocking chair and admiring the view...or take a tour boat out to the coral reef and enjoy an hour or more in the water, discovering fish and sea creatures at your own pace and under your own power. Snorkeling requires no heavy tanks and not much special gear, so even the inexperienced can enjoy a wonderful day exploring this otherwise inaccessible aquatic landscape.

If snorkeling doesn't appeal to you, you can take a glass-bottomed boat tour and see the magical ecosystem bustling below the surface. If you've never viewed the wonders of the tropical deep from the viewing gallery of a boat's transparent floor, Biscayne provides a marvelous environment for your first glimpse into the tropics' secrets.

Hours: The park is open twenty-four hours a day, seven days a week, year-round.

The visitor center is open daily year-round, from 9:00 A.M. to 5:00 P.M.

Fees: Admission to the park is free.

How to get there: From the north, take Florida's Turnpike south to exit 6 (Speedway Boulevard). Turn left off the exit ramp, and continue south to Southwest 328th Street (North Canal Drive). Turn left and continue 5 miles to the end of the road to the park entrance.

From U.S. Highway 1, drive south to Homestead. Turn left on Southwest 328th Street, (North Canal Drive), and continue 9 miles to the end of the road to the park entrance.

From the south, drive north on US 1 to Homestead. Turn right on Southwest 328th Street, and continue to the end of the road to the park entrance.

Stamping Locations and What the Cancellations Say
Dante Fascell Visitor Center

☐ Biscayne National Park/Homestead, FL **❶**

Titusville, Florida
(321) 267-1110
www.nps.gov/cana
Eastern time zone

Number of cancellations: Six

Difficulty: Challenging

About this site: Twenty-four miles of undeveloped beach grace the Florida coastline at Canaveral, where fourteen endangered or threatened animal species—the second largest number of any national park site—thrive in a protected environment. The park's 58,000 acres include wide expanses of water, sliced by a narrow barrier island that separates the Atlantic Ocean from Mosquito Lagoon, one of the most productive estuaries in Florida and a haven for nesting sea turtles, wading birds, and shellfish.

Stamping tips: Playalinda Beach closes in the days before a scheduled launch at the John F. Kennedy Space Center, and remains closed until a day after the launch takes place. Check NASA's launch schedule at www.nasa.gov/missions/highlights/schedule.html to see if your travel plans conflict with a scheduled launch. As every American knows, launches can be delayed for weather or technical considerations, so the beach may remain closed longer than expected. It's worth noting that when Playalinda Beach is open, it's a "clothing optional" area—just a friendly warning for parents traveling with children and adolescents.

Nic and I visited the park headquarters in Titusville on the day before Thanksgiving and found that the office had closed early for the holiday. As this is a common occurrence in any business, I offer this word to the wise: Call before you travel, especially during "fringe" times before and after holidays.

This would be an easy park for stamping were it not for Eldora State House, which is only open on weekends, and Seminole Rest, for which regular hours have not yet been established. The park plans to open the historic building at Seminole Rest on weekends in fall, winter, and spring, with possible closures on weekends in summer when mosquitoes and other insects become too pesky for a pleasant visit. Call the Apollo Beach Information Center at (386) 428–3384 ext. 10 to check on the

Seminole Rest cancellation's availability. Be sure to include a Saturday or Sunday in your Canaveral plans if you want to pick up the unique cancellations at these two sites.

Don't miss this! There aren't many places where you can watch sea turtles nesting while an interpreter narrates the experience, but in June and July at Canaveral, turtle watching is a favorite pastime. So popular are trips to see loggerhead sea turtles nest that the park starts taking reservations for them in May, a month in advance of mating season. To be sure that you get a spot on a tour, call the park's main number or the seashore information center at the number above.

Yes, you guessed it: NASA's Kennedy Space Center shares a border with this park—in fact, this open land was set aside in the late 1950s to provide a buffer zone between NASA and the populated area surrounding the space center. While Playalinda Beach closes for launches, the rest of the park remains open, so if you want to feel the ground rumble as a shuttle leaves the Earth or see the rocket's gleaming arc as it slices through the atmosphere, this is a great place to do it.

Hours: Canaveral Information Center is open daily year-round, from 9:00 A.M. to 5:00 P.M. It is closed Christmas.

Eldora State House is open year-round, Friday to Sunday, from noon to 4:00 P.M.

Park headquarters in Titusville is open daily year-round, from 6:00 A.M. to 6:00 P.M. It is closed Thanksgiving, Christmas, and New Year's Day.

Merritt Island National Wildlife Refuge Visitor Information Center is open Monday to Friday from 8:00 A.M. to 4:30 P.M., Saturday from 9:00 A.M. to 5:00 P.M., and Sunday, from November to March, from 9:00 A.M. to 5:00 P.M.

Playalinda Beach Ranger Station is open daily year-round, from 6:00 A.M. to 8:00 P.M. It is closed several days before a NASA launch, reopening a day after the launch has taken place or has been scuttled.

The visitor contact area in the historic building at Seminole Rest is open sporadically on Saturday and Sunday in fall, winter, and spring, and may be closed on weekends during the summer. The area that contains the Indian shell mounds is open daily year-round, from 6:00 A.M. to sunset.

Fees: Admission is $3.00 per person per day.

How to get there: Directions are provided below to each stamping location.

Stamping Locations and What the Cancellations Say

Canaveral Information Center

Take Interstate 95 north or south to Florida 44 (exit 249). Head east on FL 44 to Florida A1A. Go south on FL A1A for 9 miles to the park entrance.
(386) 428–3384 ext. 10

☐ Canaveral National Seashore/New Smyrna Beach, FL ⓤ

Eldora State House Bookstore

7611 South Atlantic Avenue, New Smyrna Beach
(386) 428–3384
The house is located in the north district of the park. Pick up the loop road 1 mile south of the information center on FL A1A. The trail to the house begins at parking area 8 on the Eldora House loop road.

☐ Canaveral National Seashore/New Smyrna, FL ⓤ

Park headquarters

212 South Washington Avenue, Titusville
(321) 267–1110

☐ Canaveral National Seashore/Titusville, FL ⓓ

Merritt Island National Wildlife Refuge Visitor Information Center

(321) 861–0667
Located on Florida 402, 5 miles east of U.S. Highway 1 in Titusville

☐ Canaveral National Seashore/Titusville, FL ⓓ

Ranger station at the entrance to Playalinda Beach

(321) 867–4077
Take I-95 to Florida 406 (exit 220). Take FL 406 east to FL 402, and follow FL 402 east to the park entrance station.

☐ Canaveral National Seashore/Titusville, FL ⓓ

Seminole Rest

(386) 428–3384 ext. 10

From I–95, take County Road 5A (exit 231) east to US 1. Take US 1 north to the caution light in Oak Hill. Turn east onto Halifax Avenue, and continue to River Road. Turn north on River Road. Seminole Rest is 0.2 of a mile ahead, on the east side of River Road.

☐ Canaveral National Seashore/Seminole Rest ❶

The cancellation is in the historic house at the site.

🔟 Castillo de San Marcos National Monument

St. Augustine, Florida
(904) 829–6506
www.nps.gov/casa
Eastern time zone

Number of cancellations: Two

Difficulty: Easy

About this site: Before the British arrived in the New World and established Jamestown, the Spanish built the settlement of St. Augustine, establishing a colony on the site of a Timucuan Indian village in 1565. More than one hundred years later, as the value of this semitropical land began to grow, the Spanish constructed Castillo de San Marcos to protect their village, the waterways used by ships as they came and went from St. Augustine, and the treasure these ships carried back to Spain. The fort you see today was built in the late 1600s of coquina (a form of limestone), and probably still stands because of its strong masonry: It was the first Spanish fort to be built from stone instead of wood.

❶ Don't miss this! You'll visit many, many forts in your Passport cancellation stamp collecting travels, but Castillo de San Marcos provides a slightly different perspective from most in this region because of its Spanish heritage. Ornately decorated bronze cannons, architectural details with no defensive function, and the deeply religious sensibility demonstrated by the naming of each bastion for a different saint—all of these points come together to make this fort stand out among the more than twenty-five defensive strongholds preserved by the National Park Service throughout the country.

Hours: The castillo is open daily year-round, from 8:45 A.M. to 5:15 P.M. It is closed Christmas. The bookstore is open from 9:00 A.M. to 4:45 P.M. daily, and is closed Christmas.

Fees: Admission is $6.00 for adults and children sixteen and over, good for seven days. Children fifteen and under are free.

How to get there: From Interstate 95, take the exit for St. Augustine Historic Sites and downtown (Florida 16/exit 318). Follow FL 16 to U.S. Highway 1. Turn right on US 1, and go 2 miles to Castillo Drive. Turn left on Castillo, and continue to the traffic light. Turn right at the light. The castillo and parking lot are on the left. The castillo is located on Florida A1A in downtown St. Augustine, at 1 South Castillo Drive.

Stamping Locations and What the Cancellations Say
Castillo de San Marcos Bookstore
(904) 824–2615

☐ Castillo de San Marcos Nat'l Monument/St. Augustine, FL Ⓓ

☐ Castillo de San Marcos Nat'l Monument/St. Augustine, FL Ⓓ
There are two identical cancellations at this bookstore, one at each counter.

11 De Soto National Memorial

Bradenton, Florida
(941) 792–0458 ext. 105
www.nps.gov/deso
Eastern time zone

Number of cancellations: One

Difficulty: Easy

About this site: "Conquer, populate, and pacify…" These were the orders given to Hernando de Soto and his 600-man army as they embarked on a mission to take over La Florida in 1539, with the goal of establishing Spain as the ruling monarchy and taking all the treasure the Spaniards were certain they would find. The controversial four-year expedition that followed, however, bore no fruit whatsoever—in fact, despite De Soto's relentless quest to enslave the natives, take their food and belongings, and use them to help him find gold and riches, the result was only bloodshed, thousands of lives lost, and not a single ounce of precious metal obtained. This site preserves and retells De Soto's story at the point at which it began, on the shores of what is now Tampa Bay.

❶ Don't miss this! This is one of the sites at which the video presentation in the visitor center is an absolute must-see. The twenty-two-minute film provides an overview of De Soto's mission and the utter futility of his goals, his methods, and even the route he took to find gold and riches. Those who don't know the story will find the video particularly useful, as it pulls no punches in explaining the folly of the mission's intentions.

Hours: The site is open daily year-round, from 9:00 A.M. to 5:00 P.M. It is closed Thanksgiving, Christmas, and New Year's Day.

Fees: Admission to this park is free.

How to get there: From Interstate 75, follow Florida 64 (Manatee Avenue) west for 12 miles to Seventy-fifth Street West. Turn right (north) onto Seventy-fifth Street, and proceed 2.5 miles to the park entrance.

From Interstate 275 take exit 1, and follow U S. Highway 19 into Bradenton. Turn west onto FL 64, and follow the directions given above.

Stamping Locations and What the Cancellations Say
Visitor center

☐ De Soto National Memorial/Bradenton, FL ❶

📱 Dry Tortugas National Park

Key West, Florida
(305) 242-7700
www.nps.gov/drto
Eastern time zone

Number of cancellations: One, plus one for the Underground Railroad

Difficulty: Heroic

About this site: Islands created by coral reefs, devoid of fresh water but abundant in wildlife—these are the Dry Tortugas, bits of land 70 miles off the coast of Key West with a location so strategically advantageous that the United States military began construction of a massive fort here in 1846. Technological advances in weaponry rendered Fort Jefferson obsolete before it could be completed. Today the Dry Tortugas are well known as a top-ten hotspot for migrating birds, as well as a favorite snorkeling destination for its healthy coral reefs.

Stamping tips: To get to the cancellation, you must take one of the ferries that bring collectors, birders, and divers to Dry Tortugas on a daily basis. The ferry ride lasts two to two and a half hours, depending on which service you choose, and you'll have four hours or more at the park. The two ferry services recommended by the National Park Service both provide continental breakfast on board ship and a picnic lunch at Fort Jefferson. These high-speed catamarans minimize the motion of the ocean, but if you're prone to motion sickness, pick a calm day to visit.

If you'd like to arrive more quickly, seaplanes fly to the Dry Tortugas every morning and afternoon, and Seaplanes of Key West offers a half-day or full-day trip rate, so you can spend more time exploring the islands and less time in transit. It's forty minutes in each direction by plane, and the company provides a cooler with soft drinks for your stay on the island.

❶ **Don't miss this!** Did I mention the birding here? It's worth mentioning again! On the Dry Tortugas, you might see several species that can be found at no other point in the United States. Brown booby, masked booby (yes, these are actual birds), sooty tern, brown noddy, and black noddy all nest here; schedule your visit between late April and the end of May to see them.

Hours: Fort Jefferson and the visitor center are open during daylight hours, and close at dusk.

Fees: Admission is $10.00 for adults seventeen and older. Children 16 and under are free.

How to get there: There are no roads to Dry Tortugas National Park. It can only be reached by boat or seaplane from Key West. There is only one road to Key West: U.S. Highway 1, which follows the eastern coastline of the state of Florida to its terminus (mile 0) in Key West.

For ferry schedules, prices, and reservations, contact Sunny Days Catamarans at the intersection of Greene and Elizabeth Streets in Key West. The phone numbers are (800) 236–7937 or (305) 292–6100; you may also visit www.drytortugas.com. You can also contact Yankee Fleet, which docks at 240 Margaret Street, at (800) 634–0939 or (305) 294–7009, or visit www.yankee fleet.com/keywest.cfm.

Seaplane transportation is provided by Seaplanes of Key West, flying from Key West International Airport at 3471 South Roosevelt Boulevard. For schedules, prices, and reservations, contact (800) 950–2FLY or (305) 294–0709, or visit www.seaplanes ofkeywest.com.

Stamping Locations and What the Cancellations Say

Dry Tortugas Visitor Center Bookstore

Located on Garden Key inside Fort Jefferson`

☐ DRY TORTUGAS NATIONAL PARK/DRY TORTUGAS, FL ⓤ

☐ Dry Tortugas NP/Underground RR Freedom Network ⓤ

Homestead, Florida
(305) 242–7700
www.nps.gov/ever
Eastern time zone

Number of cancellations: Five

Difficulty: Challenging

About this site: Nowhere else in the world can you find a sub-tropical preserve like the one at the southern tip of Florida—a "river of grass," where a 120-mile-long shallow river flows freely from Lake Okeechobee to the Florida Bay. Less than a foot deep and 50 miles wide, the river is the foundation for a delicate ecosystem that provides critical habitat for many endangered species, including the Florida panther and the West Indian mana-tee. The alligator and the crocodile exist side by side, tens of thousands of birds find abundant food supplies during the annual migration, and all manner of native species grow and thrive in the sultry environment. But the encroachment of human develop-ment has resulted in drained and diverted waterways, introduced pollutants, and the invasion of non-native plant species that threaten to upset the sensitive balance in this unique wilderness.

Stamping tips: While it's possible to get all five cancellations in one day, it involves a lot of driving with no lengthy stops to enjoy what you will find—and there's a great deal to enjoy in the Ever-glades. Take two or even three days to walk the trails, take a boat ride or two into the backcountry, take the two-hour tram ride at Shark Valley, or even rent a canoe and paddle your way along one of the waterway "trails." If you're coming from Miami and points north, travel south and begin your tour of the Everglades at the Ernest Coe Visitor Center at the park entrance, south of Homestead. Continue just a few miles down the park road to the Royal Palm Visitor Center, where you'll get your second cancella-tion, and hike the Anhinga Trail, an easy walk where you'll see plenty of long-legged wading birds (possibly including the endan-gered wood stork), alligators, and perhaps some swimming mammals.

From Royal Palm, it's just more than 30 miles to the Flamingo Visitor Center, an area with overnight camping (the lodge was destroyed by Hurrican Wilma) and visitor services as well as a wide view of Florida Bay. You can book reservations for a back-country boat excursion. You may wish to spend the night at the campground before returning to the main road for the last two Everglades cancellations.

The only way to get to Shark Valley and Everglades City is by returning to the park's main entrance—38 miles from Flamingo—and taking Florida's Turnpike to U.S. Highway 41. Drive west on US 41 to Shark Valley Visitor Center, which is before Big Cypress National Preserve's Oasis Visitor Center. Shark Valley has a visitor center, restrooms, and a small pavilion at its entrance, and you can walk the trail that begins at the pavilion or take a two-hour tram ride through the northern end of the park. You may also rent bicycles and travel the 5-mile trail at your own pace.

Finally, continue west on US 41 then south on Florida 29, to Everglades City, where you'll find the Gulf Coast Visitor Center and your fifth Everglades cancellation. (From here, it's easy to continue north to De Soto National Memorial and then on to the Gulf Islands National Seashore.)

Don't miss this! Take a boat tour and go beyond the bay and the boardwalks into the backcountry to see what most people do not see when they come to the Everglades. In the less-traveled mangrove estuary, water-loving animals swim right past your boat and dolphins play in the slightly deeper waters, while birds from the swallow-tailed kite and black vulture to the endangered wood stork and the roseate spoonbill find safe haven. These narrated tours provide a local perspective on the beauty and value of this river of grass, often laced with tales of personal experiences and observations. If you are boat-touring in the Cape Sable or Flamingo areas of the park, watch for an elusive crocodile that may be disguising himself as a floating log.

Whatever you do in the Everglades, be prepared for mosquitoes and other tiny biting insects, especially from June to November. The nuisance is reduced in the dry winter months, but in spring and summer you will need long sleeves, long pants, and plenty of repellent at dawn and dusk to keep the little critters off your skin.

Hours: Ernest Coe Visitor Center is open year-round. From mid-December to mid-April, hours are from 8:00 A.M. to 5:00 P.M. From mid-April to mid-December, hours are from 9:00 A.M. to 5:00 P.M.

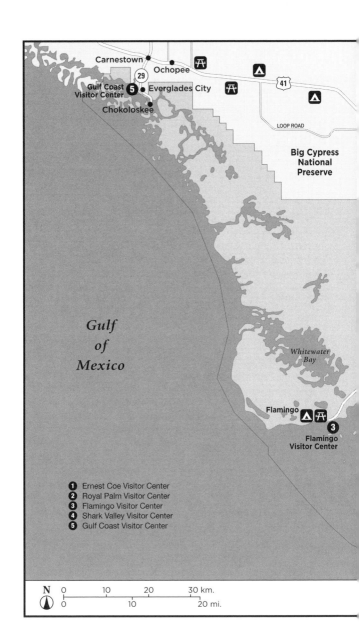

Carnestown
Ochopee
29
Everglades City
Gulf Coast 5
Visitor Center
Chokoloskee

41

LOOP ROAD

Big Cypress
National
Preserve

Gulf
of
Mexico

Whitewater
Bay

Flamingo
3
Flamingo
Visitor Center

1 Ernest Coe Visitor Center
2 Royal Palm Visitor Center
3 Flamingo Visitor Center
4 Shark Valley Visitor Center
5 Gulf Coast Visitor Center

N
0   10   20   30 km.
0   10   20 mi.

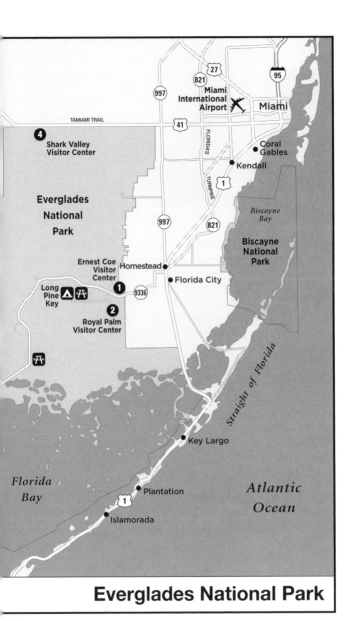

Everglades National Park

Royal Palm Visitor Center is open year-round from 8:00 A.M. to 4:15 P.M.

Flamingo Visitor Center is open from November 1 to April 30 from 8:30 A.M. to 5:00 P.M. From May 1 to October 31, the visitor center is staffed intermittently; call for hours.

Shark Valley Visitor Center is open year-round. From mid-December to mid-April, hours are from 8:45 A.M. to 5:15 P.M. From mid-April to mid-December, hours are from 9:15 A.M. to 5:15 P.M.

Gulf Coast Visitor Center is open year-round. From December 1 to mid-April, hours are from 8:00 A.M. to 4:30 P.M. From mid-April to November 30, hours are from 9:00 A.M. to 4:30 P.M.

Fees: Admission is $10.00 per vehicle, good for seven days, and $10.00 per person entering on foot or by bicycle or motorcycle, also good for seven days. Children sixteen and under are free.

How to get there: To reach the main park entrance and Flamingo from Miami, take Florida's Turnpike (Florida 821) south until it ends, merging with U.S. Highway 1 at Florida City. Turn right at the first traffic light onto Palm Drive (Florida 9336/Southwest 344th Street) and follow the signs to the park.

The Shark Valley entrance is on US 41 (Tamiami Trail) 25 miles west of Florida's Turnpike exit for Southwest Eighth Street. From the Naples area, take US 41 (Tamiami Trail) east to Shark Valley.

The Gulf Coast entrance is 5 miles south of US 41 (Tamiami Trail) on FL 29, in Everglades City. From Interstate 75 (Alligator Alley), take exit 80 (FL 29) south and proceed 20 miles to Everglades City. Once in Everglades City, follow the signs to the park. The visitor center is on the right.

Stamping Locations and What the Cancellations Say

Ernest Coe Visitor Center

40001 Florida 9336, Homestead
(305) 242–7700
Located at the main park entrance, west of Homestead and Florida City

☐ Everglades National Park/Homestead, FL ⓪

Flamingo Visitor Center

(239) 695–2945

Located 38 miles southwest of the main entrance at the southern end of the park

☐ Everglades National Park/Flamingo, FL ⓪

Gulf Coast Visitor Center

(239) 695–3311

Located on Florida's west coast in Everglades City, in the north-west corner of the park

☐ Everglades National Park/Gulf Coast, FL ⓪

Royal Palm Visitor Center

(305) 242–7700

Located on the east side of the park, 4 miles west of the main entrance station

☐ Everglades National Park/Royal Palm ⓪

Shark Valley Visitor Center

(305) 221–8776

Located on US 41 (Tamiami Trail) on the northern border of the park

☐ Everglades National Park/Shark Valley, FL ⓪

14 Florida National Scenic Trail

Headquarters in Gainesville, Florida
(877) HIKE–FLA (445-3352)
www.florida-trail.org
Eastern time zone

Number of cancellations: Two for the trail, plus two for other national park sites at trail cancellation locations

Difficulty: Tricky

About this site: One of only eight national scenic trails in the country, the Florida National Scenic Trail leads hikers from Gulf Islands National Seashore in Florida's panhandle all the way to the Loop Road in Big Cypress National Preserve. With 1,300 miles in all—including several alternative or loop routes—the trail is blazed from end to end, making it one of the most complete national scenic trails in the national park system. It passes from tropical to temperate climate as it spans the state, revealing all of Florida's charms, from wetlands filled with bromeliads to open prairie and pine woods.

Stamping tips: The hurricane seasons of 2004 and 2005 severely damaged many areas at Gulf Islands National Seashore, and repairs may take several years or longer. The Fort Pickens Visitor Center, home to one of the cancellations, and its adjacent museum are temporarily closed. The good news is that there's another cancellation at Naval Live Oaks Visitor Center in Gulf Islands National Seashore, very slightly different, so you have access to at least one imprint.

❶ Don't miss this! Whether you're looking for a pleasant walk across a broad South Florida saw grass prairie, a potentially wet exploration of cypress swamps, or a more rugged outdoor encounter in the undeveloped backcountry of the panhandle— perhaps through the Apalachicola National Forest—you will find the hidden Florida along this trail, which passes through stretches of untouched wetland, Native American reservation land, and hardwood forest that have been saved from the developer's bulldozer by the Florida Trail Association and the National Park Service.

Hours: The trail is open twenty-four hours a day, seven days a week, year-round.

Naval Live Oaks Visitor Center is open year-round from 8:30 A.M. to 4:30 P.M. It is closed Christmas.

Fort Pickens Visitor Center is temporarily closed. It will reopen when Fort Pickens Road has been rebuilt. Call before visiting.

Big Cypress Visitor Center is open daily year-round, from 9:00 A.M. to 4:30 P.M. It is closed Christmas.

Fees: There is no fee to use the trail.

How to get there: The trail begins in Big Cypress National Preserve and ends at the Gulf Islands National Seashore, crossing the entire state of Florida. Maps of the trail's many segments are available online at floridatrail.org. Directions to visitor centers in Gulf Islands National Seashore and the Big Cypress visitor center are provided in the Stamping Locations section.

Stamping Locations and What the Cancellations Say

Naval Live Oaks Visitor Center

Gulf Islands National Seashore

(850) 934–2600

Located off of U.S. Highway 98. From Pensacola, travel on US 98 south to Gulf Breeze. Continue east on US 98 to Naval Live Oaks.

☐ Gulf Islands National Seashore/FLA NS Trail **Ⓤ**

☐ Gulf Islands National Seashore/Naval Live Oaks **Ⓤ**

Fort Pickens Visitor Center

(850) 934–2635

Temporarily closed while Fort Pickens Road is rebuilt. Cancellations are unavailable until that time.

☐ Gulf Islands National Seashore/FL NS Trail **Ⓓ**

☐ Gulf Islands Nat'l Seashore/Fort Pickens **Ⓓ**

Big Cypress Visitor Center

33100 Tamiami Trail East

(239) 695–1201

Located on U.S. Highway 41 (Tamiami Trail) in southern Florida

☐ Big Cypress/Fla NS Trail **Ⓤ**

☐ Big Cypress National Preserve/Ochopee, FL **Ⓤ**

15 Fort Caroline National Memorial and Timucuan Ecological and Historic Preserve

Jacksonville, Florida

(904) 641–7155

www.nps.gov/foca, www.nps.gov/timu

Eastern time zone

Number of cancellations: Five

Difficulty: Easy

About this site: While the Spanish claimed the area we now know as Florida for Spain in 1513, France was not far behind. The French Huguenots built a colony here in 1564, calling it "La Caroline," and constructed an earthwork fort as a stronghold against the inevitable conflict with Spain. In 1565, the Spanish attacked, and in a battle that lasted just one hour, Spain triumphed over the French.

The Timucua, or "people of the shell mounds," lived in this area, a native population discovered by explorer Jean Ribault when he landed on these shores in 1562. No Timucua have survived to the present day, but history indicates that they lived in a well-organized tribal system with defined social strata, strong religious beliefs, and construction skills that were critical to the French colonists' survival in the New World.

Stamping tips: The Ribault Club, built in 1928 and reopened in 2003, was once the playground of the very rich and is now a tourist attraction. It's not open on Monday or Tuesday, but on any other day of the week you can secure your cancellation in the bookstore.

Don't miss this! Kingsley Plantation offers an overview of plantation living on a 1,000-acre sea island that once housed more than 80 slaves. The slave quarters are rare ruins of actual cabins used by Kingsley's work force, with one cabin fully restored to give visitors an idea of the meager living conditions these slaves endured.

Hours: The national memorial is open daily year-round, from 9:00 A.M. to 5:00 P.M. It is closed Thanksgiving, Christmas, and New Year's Day.

Kingsley Plantation is open daily year-round, from 9:00 A.M. to 5:00 P.M. It is closed Thanksgiving, Christmas, and New Year's Day.

Ribault Club is open Wednesday to Sunday from 9:00 A.M. to 5:00 P.M. It is closed Monday and Tuesday, and on Thanksgiving, Christmas, and New Year's Day.

Fees: Admission is free.

How to get there: From Interstate 95 north of Jacksonville, exit onto Florida 9A (exit 362A). FL 9A crosses the Saint Johns River via the Napoleon Bonaparte Broward Bridge. Exit FL 9A at Monument Road, turn left, and follow the brown signs to the memorial.

From I–95 south of Jacksonville, exit at FL 9A. Proceed to the Monument Road exit. Turn right and follow the brown signs to the memorial. The entrance to the fort is on your left at 12713 Fort Caroline Road.

To reach Kingsley Plantation, at 11676 Palmetto Avenue in Jacksonville, from I–95 north of Jacksonville, exit at FL 9A (exit 362). Leave FL 9A at Heckscher Drive (Florida 105) and turn left. In 10.5 miles, the Saint Johns River Ferry landing will be on your right. Continue 0.5 mile and turn left onto Fort George Road at the National Park Service sign. Follow the signs to the plantation.

To reach the plantation from I–95 south of Jacksonville, leave the interstate at the FL 9A exit. Continue north on FL 9A across the Saint Johns River via the Napoleon Bonaparte Broward Bridge. After crossing the bridge, take the first exit, turning right (north) on Heckscher Drive/FL 105. Travel 10.5 miles on Heckscher Drive. Pass the Saint Johns River Ferry landing on your right, continue 0.5 mile, and turn left on Fort George Road at the brown National Park Service sign. Follow the signs to the plantation.

Stamping Locations and What the Cancellations Say

Fort Caroline Visitor Center

☐ Fort Caroline National Memorial/Jacksonville, FL **①**
☐ Timucuan Preserve/Jacksonville, FL **①**

Kingsley Plantation

(904) 251–3537

☐ Kingsley Plantation, Timucuan Preserve/Jacksonville, FL **①**
☐ Kingsley Plantation, Timucuan Preserve/
   Ft. George Island, FL **①**

Ribault Club

11241 Fort George Road, Fort George Island
(904) 251–3303
Follow the directions to Kingsley Plantation above. Once on Fort George Island, pass the turn to Kingsley Plantation and continue straight on the paved road. Follow the signs to the Ribault Club.

☐ Ribault Club Timucuan Preserve/Fort George Island, FL **①**

16 Fort Matanzas National Monument

St. Augustine, Florida
(904) 471–0116
www.nps.gov/foma
Eastern time zone

Number of cancellations: One

Difficulty: Easy

About this site: Built by the Spanish between 1740 and 1742 to guard the Matanzas Inlet, Fort Matanzas stands on the site of a bloody massacre that took place in 1565, when Spanish troops overwhelmed French colonists and slaughtered hundreds of them to preserve Spanish sovereignty in this corner of the New World. The fort's major battles took place in 1741 and 1742, when Spanish colonists thwarted British attempts to take the inlet. While the fort continued to serve as a rest stop and information station for passing Spanish ships, its weapons were never fired again. Britain finally acquired Florida, and the fort, through a treaty in 1763.

Stamping tips: The cancellation is in the Fort Matanzas Visitor Center on the mainland, so you don't need to visit the fort itself. This is important because the ferry is in dry dock for several days during the first week of every month, so a trip to the fort is not always available.

❗ Don't miss this! Even if the ferry is not running, you can still enjoy this park's natural story by walking the half-mile boardwalk trail. Stroll through a last surviving stand of coastal forest—an example of the woods that once covered many barrier islands like this one—and along the tidal estuary, the waterway in which freshwater and salt water meet to create a salt marsh in which a wide range of animal and plant species thrive. You may see nesting sea turtles, or hear the call of a great horned owl in the late afternoon. Pelicans and osprey are frequent visitors, as are marsh rabbits and raccoons at dusk.

Hours: The park is open daily year-round, from 9:00 A.M. to 5:30 P.M. It is closed Christmas.

The ferry to the fort leaves the visitor center dock from 9:30 A.M. to 4:30 P.M. on the "thirty." The tour usually lasts 45 to 50 minutes, including a ranger presentation.

Fees: Admission to this park is free.

How to get there: From Interstate 95, take exit 305 (Florida 206). Follow FL 206 east about 6 miles to Florida A1A. Turn right and follow FL A1A south for 4 miles to the park entrance on the right side of the road.

From St. Augustine, follow FL A1A south for 14 miles to the park entrance on the right, at 8635 FL A1A South.

Stamping Locations and What the Cancellations Say
Fort Matanzas Visitor Center
☐ Fort Matanzas Nat'l Monument/St. Augustine, FL ❶

17 Gulf Islands National Seashore

Gulf Breeze, Florida
(850) 934–2600
www.nps.gov/guis
Central time zone

Number of cancellations: Nine

Difficulty: Challenging

About this site: The largest of the national seashores, the Gulf Islands stretch from Cat Island in Mississippi to the eastern end of Santa Rosa Island in Florida, a 160-mile strip of shifting coastline and barrier islands that not only offer sparkling white beaches and turquoise waters, but also serve up a measure of history. Gulf Islands preserves the site of the nation's first federal tree farm, established to raise live oak timber for shipbuilding, and a proud history of national defense, with gun batteries along the coastline in operation from the 1800s until 1945. Visitors come to the seashore to wander the beaches, explore the nature trails, and absorb the military history on the islands' shores.

Stamping tips: Many of the Gulf Islands sustained heavy damage during Hurricane Ivan in 2004 and Hurricane Katrina in 2005. While many facilities have reopened, others require repairs that will take years to complete. If you plan to travel to this park in 2008 hoping to accumulate all the cancellations, you may want to consider waiting several more years before making an attempt.

It's not possible for rangers, other staff members, or volunteers to help you get cancellations in closed districts—these areas are not only damaged, but often are dangerous because of debris and unstable walls, floors, and roofs left behind by the storms. Some hiking trails are closed because trees injured during the hurricanes are now dying and falling over, making the routes particularly hazardous. As of the publication deadline for this book, Fort Pickens Visitor Center is not open, so the cancellations there are unavailable. The Gulf Islands Web site contains a current list of operating areas and their conditions. Check this, or call (805) 934-2600 before you plan your trip, and if you do go collecting here, be sensitive to the fact that this park—and its staff—have undergone considerable trauma.

Two additional cancellations are available in the Mississippi section of this park.

Don't miss this! When was the last time you sat on a pier with a fishing rod and just waited for something to bite? The Gulf Islands can give you that peaceful, languid feeling you had when you were a kid (or just last week, if fishing is your passion). Try fishing on the pier at Fort Pickens, where you don't need a salt-water fishing license but you do need to know what you're catching, as regulations govern whether you can keep many of the fish you may encounter, or whether they must be released. Do your research in advance at http://myfwc.com/marine/FWC68B.htm.

Hours: Fort Barrancas Visitor Center is open daily year-round. From March to October, hours are from 9:30 A.M. to 5:00 P.M. From November to February, hours are from 8:30 A.M. to 4:00 P.M. The center is closed Christmas.

Fort Pickens is open for self-guided tours, and the visitor center will reopen when the Fort Pickens Road has been rebuilt. Call before visiting.

Naval Live Oaks Visitor Center is open daily year-round, from 8:30 A.M. to 4:30 P.M.

Fees: Admission is $8.00 per vehicle, good for seven days. Individuals arriving on foot, bicycle, or motorcycle are charged $3.00 per person, good for seven days. There is no fee to visit the Naval Live Oak Visitor Center.

How to get there: From the east, take Interstate 10 to exit 22 and the Garcon Point Bridge. From the bridge, take U.S. Highway 98 east from Pensacola. Alternatively, take I–10 to Interstate 110, across the Three Mile Bridge, to Gulf Breeze and US 98. Directions to cancellation locations are provided below.

Stamping Locations and What the Cancellations Say

Fort Barrancas Visitor Center
(850) 455–5167

To reach the mainland forts on Pensacola Naval Air Station, use Blue Angel Parkway (Florida 173). The fort is on Taylor Road, 0.5 mile east of the Museum of Naval Aviation.

☐ Gulf Islands National Seashore/Fort Barrancas ⓤ

Naval Live Oaks Visitor Center
(850) 934–2600

The Naval Live Oaks Area is just east of Gulf Breeze on US 98.

☐ Gulf Islands National Seashore/Naval Live Oaks ⓤ

☐ Gulf Islands National Seashore/FLA NS Trail ⓤ

Fort Pickens Visitor Center
(850) 934–2635

The Fort Pickens area is on Santa Rosa Island, west of Pensacola Beach. The Fort Pickens Road is currently closed to vehicles, but visitors can walk or cycle the road. Visitors also can make arrangements with a National Park service-licensed boat captain for a water taxi to the area. Call (850) 934–2600 for information. The visitor center is currently closed and cancellations below are unavailable until it reopens.

☐ Gulf Islands Nat'l Seashore/Fort Pickens ⓤ

☐ Gulf Islands National Seashore/FL NS Trail ⓤ

Fort Pickens Entrance Station

Closed due to hurricane damage

☐ Gulf Islands National Seashore/Fort Pickens **Ⓓ**

Fort Pickens Campground Registration

Closed due to hurricane damage

☐ Gulf Islands National Seashore/Fort Pickens **Ⓓ**

Perdido Key Entrance Station

Florida 292 leads southwest from Pensacola to the Perdido Key area. On the island, turn left onto Johnson Beach Road.

☐ Gulf Islands National Seashore/Perdido Key **Ⓤ**

Santa Rosa Entrance Station

Closed to vehicles due to hurricane damage and road reconstruction

☐ Gulf Islands National Seashore/Santa Rosa **Ⓤ**

Georgia

18 Andersonville National Historic Site

Andersonville, Georgia
(229) 924–0343
www.nps.gov/ande
Eastern time zone

Number of cancellations: One

Difficulty: Easy

About this site: More than 45,000 Union prisoners spent their captivity in Andersonville in 1864 and 1865, enduring or perishing in conditions that included exposure to heat and cold, poor sanitation, malnutrition, and the rampant spread of disease. In the fourteen months of this camp's operation, 12,920 prisoners died at Andersonville, as the numbers of inmates became impossible for the Confederate management to feed and house. Today Andersonville stands as a monument to the brave men and women who served, suffered, and died on these grounds, while the National Prisoner of War Museum provides historical and global perspective on prisoners of all wars since our nation began.

Don't miss this! The National Prisoner of War Museum, which opened in 1998, is one of the most well-planned and informative museums in the national park system. This remarkable museum takes an extremely uncomfortable and disturbing subject and presents it without resorting to shock or pedantics. Instead, it tells the compelling human stories of experiences shared by thousands of prisoners in every war in which America has played a role since the Revolution. Living conditions, food, clothing, comradeship in the face of adversity, sanity-preserving pastimes, and the eventual return to the free world all receive even-handed attention.

When you're ready to drive the park loop road, the park's audio tour (available for a nominal fee) guides you through the prison site and national cemetery.

Hours: The site is open daily year-round, from 8:30 A.M. to 5:00 P.M. It is closed Thanksgiving, Christmas, and New Year's Day.

Fees: Admission to this park is free.

How to get there: The park is in Andersonville, about 10 miles north of Americus, at 496 Cemetery Road.

From north Georgia, follow Interstate 75 south to exit 149 for Georgia 49. Follow GA 49 south through Fort Valley, Marshallville, Montezuma, and Oglethorpe, and continue for another 10 miles to the park entrance, which is on the left.

From south Georgia, follow I–75 north to exit 101 for U.S. Highway 280 (near Cordele). Follow US 280 west to Americus. Turn right onto GA 49, heading north to Andersonville. The park entrance is on the right, about 10 miles north of Americus.

Stamping Locations and What the Cancellations Say
Andersonville Visitor Center

☐ Andersonville National Historic Site/Andersonville, GA ⓞ

🔢 Augusta Canal National Heritage Area

Georgia NPS Affiliated Site
Augusta, Georgia
(888) 659–8926
www.augustacanal.com
Eastern time zone

Number of cancellations: One

Difficulty: Easy

About this site: The only southern industrial canal that's still intact and in continuous use, the Augusta Canal opened in 1846 and has served as a source of hydropower and clean water as well as a commercial and pleasure boat route. Just as city planners hoped when they ordered its construction, the canal brought industrial expansion to Augusta as textile mills and ironworks sprang up along its banks, turning the city into a boomtown in the mid- to late 1800s. In the 1970s, interest rose in preserving this important part of Augusta's history, eventually leading to the canal's designation as a national heritage area.

Stamping tips: As the Augusta Canal Interpretive Center is open daily year-round, you'll have no trouble getting this cancellation. Note the later opening time on Sunday. If you're in a hurry, you don't need to pay admission and tour the center to get the cancellation (it's at the front desk, where you buy center/boat tour tickets and pay for gift shop purchases), but this picturesque location may lure you to enjoy a pleasant boat trip or wander the displays before you run off to your next stop.

Don't miss this! With quiet waters and mostly undeveloped, natural areas along the Fall Line (the environmental line between the granite plateau and the coastal plain), the Augusta Canal simply begs to be enjoyed from the deck of a tour boat. Petersburg Boats carry forty-nine passengers on open decks, providing plenty of viewing space and lively running commentary by well-versed narrators. The boats run year-round, and you have your choice of an hour-long cruise or a three-hour excursion, as well as a sunset cruise (times vary by season). Call the interpretive center for boat launch times and prices.

Hours: The Augusta Canal Interpretive Center is open year-round, Monday to Saturday from 9:30 A.M. to 5:30 P.M., and Sunday from 1:00 P.M. to 5:30 P.M. It is closed on federal holidays.

Fees: Admission to the center is $6.00 for adults, $4.00 for seniors over sixty-five, active military personnel, and students in prekindergarten through high school or college with valid identification, and free for children under four. Basic boat tour tickets are $12.00 and include free admission to the interpretive center.

How to get there: From Interstate 20, take exit 200 for Riverwatch Parkway. Turn left on Riverwatch Parkway, and continue 5 miles to Thirteenth Street. Turn right on Thirteenth Street, then right on Greene Street to Enterprise Mill.

From Riverwalk area/Cotton Exchange: Take Reynolds Street westbound to Thirteenth Street. Turn left on Thirteenth Street. At the second traffic light, turn right. Travel approximately 0.3 mile to Enterprise Mill. The entrance is on the west (far) side of the mill.

Stamping Locations and What the Cancellations Say

Augusta Canal Interpretive Center
Enterprise Mill, 1450 Greene Street #400
(706) 823–0440 ext. 4

☐ Augusta Canal National Heritage Area/Augusta, GA **❶**
The cancellation is at the front desk (ticketing/gift shop).

20 Chattahoochee River National Recreation Area

Atlanta, Georgia
(678) 538–1200
www.nps.gov/chat
Eastern time zone

Number of cancellations: One

Difficulty: Easy

About this site: Right in the heart of Atlanta, in the last place you'd expect to find a natural area preserved as a national park site, the Chattahoochee River flows freely and its banks remain wild and undeveloped. It's held in place by the Brevard Fault, the natural dividing line between the Appalachian and Piedmont regions, which has kept the river on its current course for centuries while ensuring a forever-wild landscape of hills, valley, shoals, and thick woods. This 48-mile stretch of the river's total 542 miles is carefully managed as a source of drinking water for Atlanta residents, a constant battle to keep it free of pollutants from agricultural and industrial endeavors.

❶ Don't miss this! This recreation area has nine units, each with its own offerings for hiking, boating, swimming, fishing, and camping. More than 50 miles of hiking trails range from easy strolls through the woods to challenging hikes along steep, rocky bluffs. Follow the "hiking" links on the park's Web site for maps and details on each trail. If you've got your bicycle, a 3-mile loop on Cochran Shoals takes you through the wetlands on a level, hard-packed pathway, with plenty of opportunities to view birds and wildlife.

Hours: The park is open daily year-round, from 9:00 A.M. to 5:00 P.M. It is closed Christmas.

Fees: Admission to the park is free. A $3.00 fee per vehicle is charged for parking.

How to get there: To reach the Island Ford Visitor Center from northbound Georgia 400, take exit 6 (Northridge Road). Stay in the right lane, cross over GA 400, and turn right onto Dunwoody Place. Go 0.5 mile to Roberts Drive. Turn right and proceed 0.7 mile to Island Ford Parkway and the park entrance on your right.

From southbound GA 400, take exit 6 (Northridge Road). Continue straight ahead at the traffic light onto Dunwoody Place. Go 0.5 mile to Roberts Drive. Turn right and proceed 0.7 mile to the park entrance on your right.

Stamping Locations and What the Cancellations Say

Island Ford Visitor Center
1978 Island Ford Parkway
(678) 538–1200

☐ Chattahoochee River NRA/Atlanta, GA ⓪

21 Chickamauga and Chattanooga National Military Park

Fort Oglethorpe, Georgia
(706) 866–9241
www.nps.gov/chch
Eastern time zone

Number of cancellations: One in Georgia. An additional cancellation for this park is available at Lookout Mountain in Tennessee.

Difficulty: Easy

About this site: The 1863 Campaign for Chattanooga—one of the hardest fought in the Civil War—began in June 1863 and included two principal battles, the Battle of Chickamauga (September 18 to 20) and the Battle for Chattanooga (November 23 to 25). More than 150,000 Union and Confederate soldiers wrestled—sometimes literally—for control of Chattanooga, an important railroad hub and gateway to the Confederate military-industrial heartland. Brilliant military strategy on the part of the Union Army of the Cumberland forced the Confederates to abandon Chattanooga without a fight, but as winter approached in

November, the Union attempted to advance, and 34,000 men became casualties in three bloody days of fighting. Defeated Union forces were forced to retreat into Chattanooga. The Confederate Army of Tennessee attempted to besiege the Union forces in Chattanooga, but the arrival of re-enforcements and a new commander, General Ulysses S. Grant, allowed the Federals to break out and drive the Confederates from Lookout Mountain and Missionary Ridge, establishing Union control in advance of the drive across Georgia the following year.

Don't miss this! So much struggle took place on these grounds that the video and displays in the visitor center only begin to address the true scope of the campaign. Once you have begun to grasp the enormity of the conflict, take one of the self-guided tours around the battlegrounds. In season, go on a ranger-led tour. The stories of tiny incremental gains after hours of combat, coupled with the conditions under which these men waited, slept, prepared for battle, fought, and lived or died, will leave you with an entirely appropriate sense of awe at the commitment of the men on both sides of the cause.

Hours: The grounds are open daily from dawn to dusk. The visitor center is open daily year-round, from 8:30 A.M. to 5:00 P.M. It is closed Christmas.

Fees: Admission to this park is free.

How to get there: Chickamauga Visitor Center is located 1 mile south of the intersection of LaFayette Road with Georgia 2 (Battlefield Parkway) and U.S. Highway 27 in Fort Oglethorpe.

Stamping Locations and What the Cancellations Say

Chickamauga Battlefield Visitor Center Bookstore
(706) 866–9241

☐ ChChNMP Chickamauga Battlefield/Ft. Oglethorpe, GA **❶**

22 Cumberland Island National Seashore

St. Marys, Georgia
(912) 882–4336 ext. 254
www.nps.gov/cuis
Eastern time zone

Number of cancellations: Three

Difficulty: Easy

About this site: Nothing between you and the sea but salt marsh, mudflats, and sand—that's what you'll find on Cumberland Island, the largest and southern-most of Georgia's barrier islands. Pine and hardwood forests protect the mainland shore from salt spray and provide habitat for white-tailed deer, raccoons, and armadillos, while the salt marshes and mudflats support all manner of sea and shorebirds, loggerhead sea turtles, shellfish, and indigenous plants.

Stamping tips: All cancellations are accessible every day, but to get the cancellation at Sea Camp, you must take the ferry to the island. There are plenty of good reasons to visit this island's peaceful beaches and wilderness trails and to spend a day biking, walking, picnicking, or reading a good book on the sand, but the cancellation on the island is a duplicate of the one you'll get at the Mainland Museum, so the ferry ride is not absolutely necessary.

Don't miss this! Wildlife watching is a favorite pastime on this island, as the animals and birds roam freely among the ruins of historic buildings, on the beaches, and through the woods. You're likely to spot wild horses on the beach or mudflats, as well as white-tailed deer, wild turkeys, sea turtles, and a scurrying armadillo. You may also see flocks of sandpipers and plovers, as well as herons, egrets, and other long-legged wading birds. You'll get a great view of the salt marshes from the Dungeness Marsh Boardwalk and from vantage points farther north on the island. But you'll have to walk to see all the sights, so wear comfortable shoes and bring bug spray.

Hours: The Cumberland Island National Seashore Visitor Center is open daily year-round, from 8:00 A.M. to 4:30 P.M. The center is closed Christmas.

The Mainland Museum is open daily year-round, from 1:00 to 4:00 P.M. It is closed Christmas and New Year's Day.

Sea Camp Ranger Station is open daily year-round, from 8:00 A.M. to 4:30 P.M. It is closed Christmas.

Fees: Admission is $4.00 per person, and free to children 15 and under. The round-trip ferry ticket is $17.00 for adults, $12.00 for children 12 and under, and $15.00 for seniors 65 and older.

How to get there: Cumberland Island is located 7 miles off the southeastern coast of Georgia and is accessible by boat or by a concession-operated passenger ferry. The ferry departs St. Marys daily at 9:00 A.M. and 11:45 A.M., and returns from Cumberland Island at 10:45 A.M. and 4:45 P.M. An additional ferry runs from the island Wednesday through Sunday between March 1 and October 1, departing at 2:45 P.M. Call the Cumberland Queen ferry company for reservations at 877–860–6787.

To reach the visitor center in St. Marys, take exit 3 off of Interstate 95, turn left, and follow Georgia 40 to its end. Turn right; the visitor center is on the left.

Stamping Locations and What the Cancellations Say

Cumberland Island National Seashore Visitor Center
St. Marys
(912) 882–4336 ext. 254
☐ CUMBERLAND ISLAND NS/ST. MARYS, GA **❶**

Mainland Museum
129 Osborne Street, St. Marys
(912) 882–4336
☐ Cumberland Island NS/St. Marys, Ga **❶**

Sea Camp Ranger Station
Located at the Sea Camp Dock on Cumberland Island
☐ Cumberland Island NS/St. Marys, Ga **❶**

23 Fort Frederica National Monument

Saint Simons Island, Georgia
(912) 638–3639
www.nps.gov/fofr
Eastern time zone

Number of cancellations: One

Difficulty: Easy

About this site: We now call it Georgia, but in the early eighteenth century, the land between South Carolina and Florida was known to British and Spanish colonists as the "debatable land," soil over which the two nations battled for many decades. While the Spanish established two Franciscan missions on Saint Simons Island in the 1600s, England claimed the land and constructed a colony in 1733, building Fort Frederica in 1736 to guard against the inevitable Spanish attack. Sure enough, the Spanish forces arrived in 1742, but were thwarted by the well-prepared British, cementing Britain's position as the sovereign of this land.

Don't miss this! Precious little remains of Fort Frederica and the town it protected—some building foundations and archaeologists' calculations that helped locate streets and lot lines—so to appreciate the slice of history that took place here, spend some time in the visitor center and see the video. *Fort Frederica: History Uncovered* tells the story of the archaeological dig that revealed these ruins, while providing background on the people and the battles that shaped Frederica Town.

Hours: The fort is open daily year-round, from 9:00 A.M. to 5:00 P.M. It is closed Christmas.

Fees: Admission is $3.00 for adults, good for seven days. Children fifteen and under are free.

How to get there: From U.S. Highway 17 in southeastern Georgia, take the F. J. Torras Causeway to Saint Simons Island. At the first traffic light, turn left onto Sea Island Road. Go 1.5 miles to the traffic light, and turn left onto Frederica Road. Follow Frederica Road for 2 miles, and take the second right off the roundabout. The park entrance is 300 yards past Christ Church, at 6515 Frederica Road.

Stamping Locations and What the Cancellations Say

Fort Frederica Visitor Center

☐ Fort Frederica National Monument/St. Simons Island, GA ❶

24 Fort Pulaski National Monument

Savannah, Georgia
(912) 786–5787
www.nps.gov/fopu
Eastern time zone

Number of cancellations: One, plus one for the Underground Railroad

Difficulty: Easy

About this site: It took eighteen years and $1 million in the mid-1800s for the U.S. government to build Fort Pulaski, one of more than thirty forts constructed to guard the nation's eastern coastline with the era's highest level of structural strength and durability. Before Fort Pulaski could be properly armed and readied for battle, however, it became the property of the Confederate government when Georgia seceded from the Union—and within a year, the United States Army found itself attacking the very fort it had built and fortified. Imagine their surprise, then, when ten new experimental rifled cannons acquired by the Union blasted right through Pulaski's walls! The demoralized Confederate commander surrendered soon after the walls fell, ending the bombardment and the useful life of Fort Pulaski.

❶ **Don't miss this!** You can tour this fort on your own, but the ranger-guided tours feature musket demonstrations, soldiers in uniform, and a great deal of historical perspective. If nineteenth-century military lore is your passion, you must arrive on the hour between 11:00 A.M. and 4:00 P.M. for a guided program with a ranger or skilled volunteer.

Hours: The fort is open daily year-round. Fall, winter, and spring hours are from 9:00 A.M. to 5:00 P.M. daily. Extended summer hours for the Fort Pulaski Visitor Center are from 9:00 A.M. to 6:00 P.M.; the fort is open from 9:00 A.M. to 6:30 P.M. It is closed Thanksgiving and Christmas.

Fees: Admission is $7.00 for adults and children sixteen and older. Children fifteen and younger are free.

How to get there: From Savannah, follow U.S. Highway 80 east toward Tybee Island. The entrance is located about 15 miles east of Savannah.

Stamping Locations and What the Cancellations Say
Fort Pulaski Visitor Center

☐ Fort Pulaski Nat'l Monument/Cockspur Island, GA ❶

☐ Fort Pulaski NM/Underground RR Freedom Network ❶

25 Jimmy Carter National Historic Site

Plains, Georgia
(229) 824–4104
www.nps.gov/jica
Eastern time zone

Number of cancellations: One

Difficulty: Easy

About this site: The thirty-ninth president of the United States hailed from Plains, Georgia, where he grew up the son of a farmer and learned solid values instilled by his family, the Baptist church, and his schoolteachers. Jimmy Carter ran his successful 1976 presidential campaign from a train depot not far from the local high school, and his ties to his hometown remain as strong today as they were when he was a child on the family farm.

Plains High School serves as the visitor center for the Jimmy Carter National Preservation District, with displays on the president's life before politics, his career as governor of Georgia, his presidency, and his effectiveness as an international negotiator for peace. Tour the Carters' farm and hear the president talk about his childhood in his own words, in recorded messages throughout the farm buildings.

❶ **Don't miss this!** Here's an experience you'll find nowhere else: When he and the former first lady are home in Plains, President Carter himself actually teaches Sunday school at Maranatha Baptist Church in town. You are welcome to attend and enjoy this extraordinary opportunity to visit with President Carter, a rare chance to see a living president in person in an informal setting. Call the visitor center for the dates on which Mr. Carter is expected to teach.

Hours: The site is open daily year-round, from 9:00 A.M. to 5:00 P.M. It is closed Thanksgiving, Christmas, and New Year's Day.

Fees: Admission to this park is free.

How to get there: From Interstate 75, take exit 109 and travel west on Georgia 27 approximately 35 miles to Plains. Follow the national park signs to the visitor center at 300 North Bond Street.

Stamping Locations and What the Cancellations Say

Plains High School Museum and Visitor Center

☐ Jimmy Carter National Historic Site/Plains, GA ❶

26 Kennesaw Mountain National Battlefield Park

Kennesaw, Georgia
(770) 427–4686 ext. 0
www.nps.gov/kemo
Eastern time zone

Number of cancellations: One

Difficulty: Easy

About this site: For two pivotal weeks in June and July 1864, Major General William T. Sherman led 100,000 Union troops against General Joseph E. Johnston's 65,000-man Confederate army in a battle for access to Atlanta. Despite greater manpower, Sherman struggled to get through the Confederates' entrenched lines on Kennesaw Mountain. His efforts initially failed, as did a concerted frontal attack. But when he achieved some success with a diversionary tactic, he switched to a maneuvering strategy over combat, finally outflanking Johnston's army on July 2. Two months later, after heavy fighting on a series of fronts, the Union took Atlanta on September 2.

❶ **Don't miss this!** In addition to the informative eighteen-minute video and the expanded exhibits in the new visitor center (which opened in 2002), a walk or drive to the top of Kennesaw Mountain provides an expansive look at the surrounding terrain, displaying in an instant the advantages of holding this mountain as a strategic position in wartime. Beyond the Civil War insights to be gained, the view of the northern Georgia landscape before you is worth the climb (and more than worth the drive). If you choose to hike, it's a significant 700-foot incline from the visitor center to the summit, over roughly 1.2 miles of trail, and a little less steep if you walk up the road (1.4 miles).

Hours: The park is open daily year-round, from 8:30 A.M. to 5:00 P.M. eastern standard time, and 8:30 A.M. to 6:00 P.M. on weekends during daylight savings time. It is closed Thanksgiving, Christmas, and New Year's Day.

Fees: Admission to the park is free. There is a small fee for the shuttle bus ride to the top of the mountain, which is available on weekends and holidays; see the park's Web site for current pricing.

How to get there: Take Interstate 75 to exit 269 (Barrett Parkway). At the light, turn west onto Barrett Parkway. Travel down Barrett Parkway for approximately 3 miles, and turn left at the light onto old U.S. Highway 41. Turn right at the next light, onto Stilesboro Road. The visitor center is immediately on the left, at 900 Kennesaw Mountain Drive.

Stamping Locations and What the Cancellations Say
Kennesaw Mountain Visitor Center

☐ Kennesaw Mountain Nat'l Battlefield Park/Kennesaw, GA **①**

27 Martin Luther King, Jr. National Historic Site

Atlanta, Georgia
(404) 331–5190
www.nps.gov/malu
Eastern time zone

Number of cancellations: Two

Difficulty: Easy

About this site: This is Sweet Auburn, the central African-American neighborhood in Atlanta where Dr. Martin Luther King Jr. was born, lived until he was twelve years old, and then returned in 1960 to become the copastor of Ebenezer Baptist Church with his father.

Dr. King became the leader of the civil rights movement in the late 1950s and 1960s, using the tenets of peaceful, non-violent demonstration to bring attention to the need to establish fundamental human rights for African Americans throughout the nation. As he said in 1963, in his most famous speech, King dreamed of a day when "my four children will live in a nation where they will be judged not by the color of their skin, but by the content of their character."

❶ Don't miss this! The six buildings that are open to the public in this historic preservation district provide ample opportunities to get to know Dr. King on a personal level, allowing you to see the foundations on which he constructed the values that would inspire millions to admire and follow him. The modest home in which he was born, the pulpit from which he called for peaceful change, and the center built in his honor all serve as clues to the man as well as the mission. Walk this proud neighborhood and see the vibrant surroundings that helped shape King's belief that every person, regardless of ethnicity, deserves a fair chance to live in a world that supports his or her rights, ambitions, and dreams.

Hours: The visitor center is open daily year-round. During winter, spring, and autumn, hours are from 9:00 A.M. to 5:00 P.M. During the summer season (June 15 to August 15), hours are from 9:00 A.M. to 6:00 P.M. The center is closed Thanksgiving, Christmas, and New Year's Day.

Firestation #6 is open from 9:00 A.M. to 5:00 P.M. in winter, spring, and autumn. In the summer season (June 15 to August 15), it is open from 9:00 A.M. to 6:00 P.M. It is closed Thanksgiving, Christmas, and New Year's Day.

Fees: Admission to the park is free.

How to get there: From Interstates 75 and 85, northbound or southbound, take exit 248C/Freedom Parkway. Turn right at the first traffic light, on Boulevard, and at the next traffic light turn right onto John Wesley Dobbs Avenue. The visitor parking lot is on the left.

From Interstate 20 eastbound or westbound, exit at I–75/85 northbound, and follow the directions given above.

Stamping Locations and What the Cancellations Say

Visitor center
450 Auburn Avenue Northeast
(404) 331–5190 ext. 3017

☐ Martin Luther King, Jr. National Historic Site/Atlanta, GA Ⓞ

Firestation # 6
39 Boulevard Northeast
(404) 525–7557
Located at the corner of Auburn and Boulevard. Turn right as you leave the visitor center, then left on Auburn Avenue. The fire station is on the next corner, on your right.

☐ Martin Luther King, Jr. National Historic Site/Atlanta, GA Ⓞ

28 Ocmulgee National Monument

Macon, Georgia
(478) 752–8257
www.nps.gov/ocmu
Eastern time zone

Number of cancellations: One

Difficulty: Easy

About this site: Two ceremonial mounds, one burial and an earth lodge are remnants of the Mississippians, a complex Native American culture that established a community on this site sometime between c.e. 900 and 1200. The people of the Mississippian culture lived along rivers throughout the eastern United States, building enormous earthworks like these for use as funeral mounds, ceremonial platforms, and the foundations for high buildings.

They sustained an agricultural economy, growing corn, beans, and squash, and the remains of their village indicate grand ceremonial events celebrated in a huge earthen lodge (reconstructed in the 1930s). With the arrival of Hernando De Soto and his gold-seeking expedition of the mid-1500s, the native villages were destroyed and populations dwindled as European diseases ran rampant.

Don't miss this! While the visitor center and museum's main focus is on the period from about A.D. 900 to 1150, one of the most important finds was the first evidence east of the Mississippi River of the civilizations that came before that time—the Clovis Paleo-Indians who inhabited the land before 10,000 B.C.E. Hunter-gatherers who relocated as they depleted the useful resources in a given area, the Clovis never stayed long in one place, so they didn't build structures or make any major impact on the land. Only their distinctive spear points remained to indicate that they once roamed these lands. You can see the first Clovis point found in the eastern United States in Ocmulgee's interpretive center.

Hours: The monument is open daily year-round, from 9:00 A.M. to 5:00 P.M. It is closed Christmas and New Year's Day.

Fees: Admission to this park is free. A special event fee is charged for the lantern-light tour in spring, and for the Ocmulgee Indian Festival on the third weekend in September ($5.00 for visitors 13 and older; $2.00 for children 6 to 12).

How to get there: The monument is on the east side of Macon on U.S. Highway 80 (Emery Highway). Reach the highway by traveling Interstate 75 to Interstate 16 eastbound, at the north end of Macon. Take the second exit from I–16 (Coliseum exit), and follow the signs for 1.6 miles to the site.

Stamping Locations and What the Cancellations Say

Visitor center
1207 Emery Highway, Macon
☐ Ocmulgee National Monument/Macon, GA ❶

Kentucky

29 Abraham Lincoln Birthplace National Historical Park

Hodgenville, Kentucky
(270) 358–3137
www.nps.gov/abli
Eastern time zone

Number of cancellations: Two

Difficulty: Easy

About this site: Abraham Lincoln, sixteenth president of the United States and the man who freed African-American slaves with the Emancipation Proclamation, was born on February 12, 1809, in a one-room log cabin on these lands near the Sinking Spring. The remnant stump of the boundary oak, marking the boundary of the Lincolns' property, can be found 150 yards from the site of his birth, on the 116 acres of park property that was once part of the 348-acre farm at Sinking Spring, and the spring itself flows just as it did when Lincoln lived, learned, and played here.

Don't miss this! As you walk up the long marble staircase to the imposing structure at the top and enter the memorial to view the log cabin inside, remember that this is not actually the cabin in which Nancy Lincoln gave birth to baby Abraham—in fact, despite some turn-of-the-twentieth-century showmen's claims that this cabin is authentic, there has always been irrefutable evidence to the contrary. The cabin is symbolic of the one Lincoln and his family lived in at the time of his birth. Today it is an icon, representing the modest origins of a man who rose to greatness through determination and the strength of his beliefs.

Hours: The Lincoln Birthplace is open Memorial Day through Labor Day, from 8:00 A.M. to 6:45 P.M. From Labor Day through Memorial Day, hours are from 8:00 A.M. to 4:45 P.M.

The Boyhood Home is open during daylight hours year-round. The site is staffed daily from 8:30 A.M. to 4:30 P.M.

Fees: Admission to this park is free.

How to get there: Traveling north on Interstate 65, exit at Sonora (exit 81), and go east on Kentucky 84 to Kentucky 61. Turn right on KY 61, then right again at the traffic light; the park is 3 miles ahead at 2995 Lincoln Farm Road.

Traveling south on I-65, exit at Elizabethtown (exit 91), and follow KY 61 (Lincoln Parkway) south for 10 miles, then turn right at the light at the intersection of KY 61 and Kentucky 31E. The park is about 1.5 miles from the traffic light, on the right.

Stamping Locations and What the Cancellations Say

Lincoln Birthplace visitor center

☐ ABRAHAM LINCOLN BIRTHPLACE NHP/
HODGENVILLE, KY ⓘ

Ranger station at the Boyhood Home, Knob Creek Farm

(502) 549-3741

From Lexington, Kentucky, take U.S. Highway 60 west to the Martha Layne Collins Bluegrass Parkway (exit 72). Continue on Bluegrass Parkway to U.S. Highway 31 east at exit 21. Follow US 31E south for 20 miles. The unit entrance is on the right.

☐ ABRAHAM LINCOLN BIRTHPLACE NHS/BOYHOOD UNIT ⓘ

30 Big South Fork National River and Recreation Area

Stearns, Kentucky
(423) 286-7275
www.nps.gov/biso
Eastern time zone

Number of cancellations: Three in Kentucky, plus an additional cancellation in Tennessee

Difficulty: Tricky

About this site: In Kentucky, an important part of this river's heritage has been restored at the Blue Heron Mining Community, a resurrected ghost town filled with open-air steel frames constructed where town buildings once stood. A center of coal mining operations until 1962, Blue Heron was part of the Stearns Coal and Lumber Company operations—one of the companies in this region that harvested coal on the Big South Fork of the Cumberland River. Today the remains of Blue Heron's Mine 18 include audio recollections by former mining company employees and their families of the life they led here.

The recreation area stretches south into Tennessee; more information on the area is included in that chapter.

Stamping tips: While Blue Heron Mining Community is open around the clock all year, the Stearns Depot Visitor Center is closed during the winter months from December through March. Visitors are advised to call ahead to ensure staff is available. The visitor center is staffed during business hours April through October. As long as you are traveling here during these months, you will pick up the two Kentucky cancellations with ease.

Don't miss this! If you're up for a challenge, take on the 6.5-mile loop trail that begins and ends at the mining community. This moderate hike takes you through the fascinating Blue Heron ghost town and beyond to several scenic overlooks, including the overlook above Devil's Jump, the rapids on the Big South Fork of the Cumberland River. This overlook atop a cliff affords an excellent view of the Class III and IV rapids on the river. This is a great place to watch the river wander through the heavily wooded countryside, a slash of clear blue whooshing past the scattered, jagged rocks in its path. If you're not up for the full loop, the overlook is only a short distance from the mining community.

Hours: Blue Heron Mining Community is open at all times for self-guided tours. Rangers are present from 9:30 A.M. to 4:30 P.M. daily from April through October.

Stearns Depot Visitor Center is open April 1 to October 31 from 9:30 A.M. to 4:30 P.M. It is closed from December through March. Call ahead to make sure it's open when you visit.

Fees: Admission to the recreation area is free.

How to get there: To reach the Stearns Depot Visitor Center from Interstate 75, take the exit for Kentucky 92, and drive west on KY 92 about 26 miles to its junction with U.S. Highway 27. Turn right (north) on US 27, and continue until you rejoin KY 92 west, which turns to the left. Turn left at this traffic light, and drive for 1 mile. Cross the bridge, turn right, and follow the signs to the Stearns Depot Visitor Center.

To reach Blue Heron Campground, turn off US 27, and drive west on KY 92 west for about 1.3 miles, then bear left onto Country Road 1651. Continue for 1 mile, and turn right onto Kentucky 742. From KY 742, follow the brown park signs to the Blue Heron Campground, Bear Creek Horse Camp, the river gorge overlooks, or the Blue Heron Coal Mining Community.

Stamping Locations and What the Cancellations Say

Stearns Depot Visitor Center

(606) 376–5073

Located in downtown Stearns, 1.5 miles west of KY 27, in the Big South Fork Scenic Railway Depot. Go north on US 27 through Oneida to KY 92 west. Turn left at the traffic light, and go 1 mile. Cross the bridge, and turn right, then follow the signs to the Stearns Depot Visitor Center.

☐ Big South Fork Nat'l River & Rec Area/Stearns, KY **Ⓤ**

☐ Big South Fork NRRA/Blue Heron **Ⓓ**

Train Depot in Blue Heron Mining Community

(606) 376–3787

Blue Heron is located on KY 742, 9 miles west of Stearns.

☐ Big South Fork NRRA/Blue Heron **Ⓓ**

31 Cumberland Gap National Historical Park

Middlesboro, Kentucky
(606) 248–2817
www.nps.gov/cuga
Eastern time zone

Number of cancellations: Seven

Difficulty: Challenging

About this site: Wind, water, and the gradual movement of the earth over millions of years created this natural gap in the Appalachian Mountains, a pathway to the otherwise inaccessible westward lands for large game animals, Native Americans, and eventually early American settlers. Four natural features—a channel cut by Yellow Creek, the flat Middlesboro Basin, the Yellow Creek Valley, and The Narrows in Pine Mountain—all came together in exactly the right confluence to form a perfect trail, beaten into high definition by migrating buffalo and used extensively by native peoples as they accessed the salt licks and fertile lands to the west.

As many as 300,000 people used the Gap to cross into Kentucky's Bluegrass region from 1763 through about 1810, including Daniel Boone, the person most identified with this natural trail.

Stamping tips: All but one of the cancellations are available any time, which is great if you are not collecting every existing cancellation. But the unique "Middlesboro" cancellation at the information booth in the Daniel Boone parking lot (different from the "Middleboro" cancellation at the visitor center) can be collected only in the half-hour (or less) before the Gap Cave and Hensley Settlement tours, twice daily in summer (and at more limited times throughout the rest of the year). The information booth is not staffed at any other time. This means that you'll need to do some fairly careful planning to pick this one up—especially if you don't plan to take the Gap Cave or Hensley Settlement tours.

Don't miss this! This entire park is undergoing an extensive and highly successful restoration to return it to its original condition, before development and highway construction marred its beauty in the 1950s. The original Wilderness Road Trail provides visitors a chance to walk in the footsteps of Daniel Boone and hundreds of thousands of Native Americans and pioneers as they crossed this wild land in search of new homes, fertile cropland, and business opportunities.

It's only a 2.4-mile hike to Tri-State Peak, one of the few places in America where you can stand at one point and be in three states—Kentucky, Tennessee, and Virginia—at the same time. At 1,990 feet, it's an easy peak to reach, a pleasant walk from the Wilderness Road Trail (starting at the Thomas Walker parking lot) to the Tri-State Trail, near the saddle of the Cumberland Gap.

Hours: The visitor center is open daily year-round, from 8:00 A.M. to 5:00 P.M. It is closed Christmas.

The Daniel Boone parking lot information booth is open 30 minutes before tour times only. From Memorial Day to Labor Day, the booth is open daily from 9:30 to 10:00 A.M. and 1:30 to 2:00 P.M. From early September to December 31 and from April 1 to Memorial Day, the booth is open weekdays from 9:30 to 10:00

A.M., and weekends from 9:30 to 10:00 A.M. and 1:30 to 2:00 P.M. From January 1 to March 31, the booth is open weekends only from 9:30 to 10:00 A.M. and 1:30 to 2:00 P.M. It is closed all other times.

Fees: Admission to the park is free.

How to get there: From Interstate 75, take exit 25E south at Corbin. Cumberland Gap is located in Middleboro, 50 miles south of Corbin on U.S. Highway 25E.

From Interstate 81 in Tennessee, exit onto US 25E at Morristown. The park is located 50 miles northwest on US 25E.

To reach the Daniel Boone parking lot from the visitor center, take US 25E south through the tunnel to the first exit for Kentucky 58. Take KY 58 to the sign that says: HISTORIC AREA: CUMBERLAND GAP, TN. Turn left on the historic area road; the parking area is on the right.

Stamping Locations and What the Cancellations Say

Cumberland Gap Visitor Center
(606) 248–2817 ext. 4
- ☐ Cumberland Gap NHP/Gap Cave **D**
- ☐ Cumberland Gap NHP/Hensley Settlement **U**
- ☐ Cumberland Gap NHP/Pinnacle Overlook **U**
- ☐ Cumberland Gap NHP/Wilderness Road Trail **D**
- ☐ Cumberland Gap NHP/Middleboro, KY **U**

Daniel Boone parking lot information booth
(423) 869–5699
Located on North Cumberland Drive, off of the Wilderness Road (U.S. Highway 58) at the Cumberland Gap
- ☐ Cumberland Gap NHP/Middlesboro, KY **U**
- ☐ Cumberland Gap NHP/Gap Cave **D**

32 Mammoth Cave National Park

Mammoth Cave, Kentucky
(270) 758–2180
www.nps.gov/maca
Central time zone

Number of cancellations: One

Difficulty: Easy

About this site: It's the big one—the longest recorded cave system in the world, wandering through 367 miles of underground passageways (14 miles are open to the public) and opening out into colossal subterranean rooms, then narrowing into tight squeezes before reaching the next caverns with their neck-craning ceilings and striated walls. Loaded with history and local lore, Mammoth Cave goes far beyond the basic cave tour experience to provide a cultural picture of the people who lived, worked, and explored here, from the native people who discovered the cave 4,000 years ago to twentieth-century adventure, opportunism, scandal, and tragedy. There's plenty to do beyond the caves as well, with 101 miles of scenic road, more than 70 miles of horseback and hiking trails, and two rivers for fishing and canoeing.

Don't miss this! Many tours of Mammoth Cave are quite gentle when compared to cave tours in the Rocky Mountain or western states, as Mammoth offers long, sloping passageways and big, wide-open caverns. The shorter tours of Mammoth Cave stay within the most spacious and high-ceilinged areas, making them less claustrophobia-inducing than tours at smaller caves.

Don't leave this park without finding someone who will tell you the story of Floyd Collins, the veteran spelunker of the early 1920s who found himself trapped in an unexplored passage and unable to get out. The nearly two-week ordeal Collins suffered rose to a level of national attention that rivaled the Lindbergh baby kidnapping, as thousands of people descended on Cave City and turned Collins's rescue operation into a veritable carnival. You can still see the Cave City rock merchants' shops that bear signs claiming that the owners are "kinfolk of Floyd Collins," a statement that meant big business for them for decades.

Hours: The visitor center is open daily year-round. Summer hours are from 8:00 A.M. to 7:00 P.M. The center has earlier closing times in off-season months; call for specific hours. It is closed Christmas.

Fees: Admission to the park is free. Cave tour tickets range from $4.00 to $60.00, depending on the length and difficulty of the tour.

How to get there: From Louisville, take Interstate 65 south to exit 53 at Cave City. Turn right onto Kentucky 70. Continue on Kentucky 70/255 as it becomes Mammoth Cave Parkway, and take this to the visitor center at 1 Mammoth Cave Parkway.

From Nashville, Tennessee, take I–65 north to exit 48 at Park City, Kentucky. Turn left onto KY 255, which becomes Park City Road. Stay on Park City Road to the junction with Mammoth Cave Parkway. Turn left, and continue on Mammoth Cave Parkway to the visitor center at 1 Mammoth Cave Parkway.

Stamping Locations and What the Cancellations Say

Mammoth Cave National Park Visitor Center
(270) 758–2180
☐ MAMMOTH CAVE NP/MAMMOTH CAVE, KY ❶

Mississippi

33 Brices Cross Roads National Battlefield Site

Tupelo, Mississippi
(662) 680–4025 or (800) 305–7417
www.nps.gov/brcr
Central time zone

Number of cancellations: Two, plus three cancellations for other parks at the Natchez Trace Parkway Visitor Center in Tupelo

Difficulty: Tricky

About this site: The Confederacy and the Union clashed at Brices Cross Roads in a battle instigated by General William T. Sherman to detain General Nathan Bedford Forrest's orces while Sherman executed his "March to the Sea." In a one-day battle on June 10, 1864, General Forrest's army took out three Union soldiers for every Confederate life lost, breaking down the supply pipeline and confiscating guns, wagons, and ammunition. But the victory did not alter the course of the war, as supplies continued to flow to Sherman and Atlanta eventually fell.

Stamping tips: Watch out for Mondays and Sunday mornings, when the Brices Cross Roads Visitor and Interpretive Center in Baldwyn is closed. Beyond this, you'll need only a short stop—a brief detour from your travels up the Natchez Trace Parkway.

Don't miss this! This one-acre site offers an overlook on the field of battle, some interpretive material, and a single memorial statue flanked by cannons. Enjoy the tranquil landscape before you return to the parkway.

Hours: The Brices Cross Roads visitor center is open year-round, Tuesday to Saturday from 9:00 A.M. to 5:00 P.M., and Sunday from 12:30 to 5:00 P.M. It is closed Monday. The park is open daily, dawn to dusk.

Natchez Trace Parkway Visitor Center in Tupelo is open daily year-round, from 8:00 A.M. to 5:00 P.M. It is closed Christmas.

Fees: Admission to the park is free. The Brices Cross Roads visitor center is run by the City of Baldwyn; an admission fee of $3.00 for adults and $1.00 for children is charged.

How to get there: The site is 15 miles north of the Natchez Trace Parkway Visitor Center in Tupelo, and 6 miles west of the town of Baldwyn on Mississippi 370, 4 miles from U.S. Highway 45.

Natchez Trace Parkway Tupelo Visitor Center in Tupelo is at 2680 Natchez Trace Parkway, at the parkway's Mile 266.

Stamping Locations and What the Cancellations Say

Brices Cross Roads visitor center
607 Grisham Street, Baldwyn
(662) 365–3969
Located in Baldwyn near the intersection of US 45 and MS 370
☐ BRICES CROSSROADS/BALDWYN, MISSISSIPPI ⓤ

Tupelo Visitor Center
Natchez Trace Parkway, Mile 266
(662) 680–4025
☐ Brices Cross Roads Nat'l Battlefield Site/Tupelo, MS ⓤ
☐ Natchez Trace Parkway/AL, MS, TN ⓓ
☐ NATCHEZ TRACE PARKWAY/NATIONAL SCENIC TRAIL ⓓ
☐ Natchez Trace Parkway/Tupelo National Battlefield ⓤ

34 Gulf Islands National Seashore

Ocean Springs, Mississippi
(228) 875–9057
www.nps.gov/guis
Central time zone

Number of cancellations: Two; nine more for this park are available in Florida

Difficulty: Challenging

About this site: The largest of the national seashores, the Gulf Islands stretch from Cat Island in Mississippi to the eastern end of Santa Rosa Island in Florida, a 160-mile strip of shifting coast-line and barrier islands. Gulf Islands preserves the site of the first federal tree farm established to raise live oak timber for ship-building, and a proud history of national defense, with gun batteries along the coastline in operation from the 1800s to 1945. Visitors come to the seashore to wander the beaches, explore the nature trails, salt marshes, and bayous, and fish for saltwater specialties—as well as to tour the forts that stand strong on this hurricane-swept land.

Stamping tips: Passenger ferries to West Ship Island operate spring through fall and depart from the Gulfport Small Craft Harbor, located at the intersection of U.S. Highways 90 and 49.

For more information about ferry service to West Ship Island, contact Ship Island Excursions at (866) 466–7386, or check www.msshipisland.com for a complete schedule and fares.

❶ Don't miss this! Why go to West Ship Island? Two reasons: the kind of pristine, sun-drenched beaches you see in travel brochures, and a slice of history about which you may be entirely unaware.

Fort Massachusetts, begun in 1859 as part of the U.S. coastal defense system, had not reached completion when the Confederate Army seized it in 1861. The Union quickly regained control of the fort and The U.S. Army Corps of Engineers resumed its construction. The island was used by the military as a strategic point to capture New Orleans in 1862 and then as a prison camp for Confederate soldiers. The fort withstood the Hurricane Katrina storm surge in 2005—and, in fact, was the only building on West Ship Island left standing when the storm passed.

In the wake of Katrina, the buildings that were once here have disappeared but new ones are planned. In the meantime you will need to bring your own picnic, sunscreen, and anything else you may need to this suddenly undeveloped island. Temporary restrooms and a snack bar opened in 2007.

Hours: The Davis Bayou contact station is open daily year-round, from 8:30 A.M. to 4:30 P.M.

Tours of Fort Massachusetts are offered Wednesday through Saturday at 10:30 A.M., with additional tours at 1:30 P.M. on Saturday. On Sunday, the only tours are at 1:30 P.M. Tour times are approximate and may vary with the arrival of the ferry.

Fees: Admission to the Mississippi District is free. Transportation to the islands is by passenger ferry, and round-trip tickets are $22.00 for adults, $12.00 for children three to ten years old, and $20.00 for active military personnel and seniors 62 and older. Children two and under ride for free.

How to get there: To reach the seashore, use exits 50 or 57 south from Interstate 10. The Davis Bayou Area is on US 90, east of downtown Ocean Springs. The seasonal passenger ferry to West Ship Island leaves from the Gulfport Yacht Harbor near the intersection of US 90 and US 49 in Gulfport.

Stamping Locations and What the Cancellations Say

Davis Bayou temporary contact station
Ocean Springs
(228) 875–0821
Located on the site of the William M. Colmer Visitor Center, which was damaged by hurricanes

☐ Gulf Islands National Seashore/Ocean Springs, MS ⓞ

Fort Massachusetts on West Ship Island

☐ Gulf Island NS–Fort Massachusetts/West Ship Island, MS ⓞ
The cancellation is in the North Guard Room.

35 Natchez National Historical Park

Natchez, Mississippi
(601) 446–5790
www.nps.gov/natc
Central time zone

Number of cancellations: Eight, plus one cancellation for Natchez Trace Parkway

Difficulty: Easy/tricky

About this site: The oldest European settlement on the Mississippi River, Natchez served as the first capital of the Mississippi Territory and as the capital of Mississippi in its earliest years of statehood. In the early 1800s, as the cotton gin speedily turned crops into usable fiber and as steamboats made the export of cotton to the north and west a reality, Natchez became a boomtown, a city in a pivotal position where its residents made spectacular fortunes. Entrepreneurs flocked to Natchez, turned their ideas into profit, and began to build the antebellum mansions that would reflect their new lifestyles as landowners and millionaires in some of the nation's first suburban developments.

Stamping tips: The two unique cancellations are available in four places, so you will have ample opportunity to collect them. If you collect only unique cancellations and not the duplicates, you will move through this park with ease. If you collect an imprint from each existing cancellation, it's a little trickier: Watch out for the limited hours at the William Johnson House, which is open Thursday through Sunday only.

❶ Don't miss this! The grand and opulent Melrose estate, the former home of state senator John T. McMurran, is preserved with many of the original furnishings, clothing, and personal items intact, making this a particularly fine example of mansion life in the antebellum South. In sharp contrast, the simple home of William Johnson provides a fresh point of view on an African-American businessman's success when most black men in America were still slaves. Johnson owned a barbershop and bathhouse as well as his own land, and he and his wife raised ten children in this modest home, where he carefully recorded his daily activities in a diary from 1835 until his death in 1851. This now-published document reveals a great deal about the challenges faced by a former slave surrounded by slave owners.

Hours: Natchez Visitor Reception Center is open daily year-round, Monday through Saturday, from 8:00 A.M. to 5:00 P.M., and Sunday from 9:00 A.M. to 4:00 P.M. Hours may be extended in the summer.

Melrose is open daily year-round, from 8:30 A.M. to 5:00 P.M. Guided tours are offered on the hour between 9:00 A.M. and 4:00 P.M.

The William Johnson House is open year-round, Thursday through Sunday, from 9:00 A.M. to 5:00 P.M.

Fees: A ranger-guided tour of Melrose (only access to the house) is $8.00; you are welcome to tour the grounds at no charge. You don't need to pay admission to get the cancellations.

Admission to the William Johnson House is free.

How to get there: Natchez is located in southwestern Mississippi at the southern terminus of the Natchez Trace Parkway, and is easily accessed from Interstate 55, U.S. Highway 61, and U.S. Highway 84. From I–55 or US 84, take US 61 into Natchez. From US 61, take Melrose/Montebello Parkway east for 1 mile to the Melrose Estate.

Stamping Locations and What the Cancellations Say

Melrose Estate
1 Melrose Montebello Parkway, Natchez
(601) 446–7970

☐ Natchez National Historical Park/William Johnson House Ⓓ

☐ Natchez National Historical Park/Melrose Ⓓ

City visitor center
640 South Canal Street, Natchez
(601) 446–6631

☐ Natchez National Historical Park/Melrose Ⓓ

☐ Natchez National Historical Park/William Johnson House Ⓓ

☐ Natchez Trace Parkway/AL, MS, TN Ⓓ

City visitor center bookstore
640 South Canal Street, Natchez
(601) 442–7049 ext. 20

☐ Natchez National Historical Park/Melrose Ⓓ

☐ Natchez National Historical Park/William Johnson House Ⓓ

William Johnson House
210 State Street, Natchez
(601) 446-5790

☐ Natchez National Historical Park/William Johnson House Ⓓ

☐ Natchez National Historical Park/Melrose Ⓓ

36 Shiloh National Military Park

Shiloh, Mississippi
(731) 689–5696
www.nps.gov/shil
Central time zone

Number of cancellations: Two

Difficulty: Easy

About this site: On April 6 and 7, 1862, the Civil War expanded westward with the conflict at Shiloh. The battle for control of the western Confederate railway system at Corinth ended badly for the Southern troops, but both sides felt the losses, enduring more than 24,000 combined deaths, injuries, and soldiers missing in action before the bloody fighting came to an end.

You'll find the battlefield itself in Hardin County, Tennessee, while the Corinth Interpretive Center in Corinth, Mississippi, traces the entire history of this vital railroad junction town through four years of the Civil War, including the formation of the Confederacy, the dramatic 1862 siege and battle, and the area's postwar recovery.

Don't miss this! For those who love the details of military strategy, two films at the Corinth Civil War Interpretive Center provide the background you'll need to understand the significance of military events, and to understand the troop movements and fighting that led to the Union victory in the region.

Additional cancellations are available in Tennessee.

Hours: Corinth Civil War Interpretive Center is open daily year-round, from 8:30 A.M. to 4:30 P.M. It is closed Christmas.

Fees: Admission is $5.00 per vehicle, good for seven days.

How to get there: To reach Shiloh from Interstate 40, exit at Jackson, Tennessee, and take U.S. Highway 45 south. From Memphis, Tennessee, take U.S. Highway 72 east, and exit left onto Fulton Street in Corinth. Follow signs to the interpretive center on West Linden Street. From Tupelo, Mississippi, take U.S. Highway 45 north to Corinth and exit east onto US 72. Turn north on Fulton Street, continue to West Linden Street, turn left onto Linden, and continue to the interpretive center.

Stamping Locations and What the Cancellations Say

Corinth Civil War Interpretive Center

501 West Linden Street, Corinth
(662) 287–9273

- ☐ Corinth (Siege & Battle) Unit/C. W. Interpretive Center ❶
- ☐ Shiloh National Military Park/Corinth Ms Civil War Center ❶
  The Corinth cancellation is kept in a drawer under the cash register.

37 Tupelo National Battlefield

Tupelo, Mississippi
(800) 305–7417
www.nps.gov/tupe
Central time zone

Number of cancellations: One, plus three for other parks

Difficulty: Easy

About this site: Confederate Major General Nathan Bedford Forrest faced the Union troops at Tupelo when General William T. Sherman ordered an attack as part of his plan to keep Forrest in Mississippi while the Union general marched his forces through Georgia. Sherman sent Major General Andrew J. Smith and a large contingent of Union troops to detain the Confederate leader and his mounted infantry. In a three-day battle, Smith held Forrest back, and supplies continued to flow through Tennessee to Georgia, fortifying Sherman's march with guns and ammunition.

❗ Don't miss this! Like Brices Cross Roads a short distance away, the one-acre site of the Tupelo battlefield is marked symbolically with a stone monument and cannons. Make a short stop to pay your respects to the men who fought and died on these lands as you tour the Natchez Trace Parkway.

Hours: The site is open dawn to dusk.

Fees: Admission to this park is free.

How to get there: The one-acre site is within the city limits of Tupelo, on Mississippi 6 about 1.3 miles west of its intersection with U.S. Highway 45. It is 1 mile east of the Natchez Trace Parkway.

Stamping Locations and What the Cancellations Say

Tupelo Visitor Center*
Natchez Trace Parkway, Mile 266
(800) 305-7417

- ☐ Natchez Trace Parkway/Tupelo National Battlefield **Ⓤ**
- ☐ Natchez Trace Parkway/AL, MS, TN **Ⓓ**
- ☐ NATCHEZ TRACE PARKWAY/NATIONAL SCENIC TRAIL **Ⓓ**
- ☐ Brices Cross Roads Nat'l Battlefield Site/Tupelo, MS **Ⓤ**

38 Vicksburg National Military Park

Vicksburg, Mississippi
(601) 636-0583
www.nps.gov/vick
Central time zone

Number of cancellations: Two

Difficulty: Easy

About this site: It began on March 29, 1863, as General Ulysses S. Grant and the Army of the Tennessee marched through Louisiana, and it would be more than three months before surrender ended the siege at Vicksburg and broke the South's stronghold on the Mississippi River, a critical trade route blocked to the United States by Confederate forces two years earlier.

Grant had nearly three times as many men as the entrenched Confederates, and moved inland through heavy fighting at Port Gibson, Grand Gulf, Raymond, and Jackson. At Champion Hill, Grant won a decisive victory with disastrous consequences for the Confederates, yet the Southern army continued to fight, rallying at Vicksburg and holding the Union back until Grant cut off all supply lines into the city in May. Finally, exhausted by the constant bombardment and demoralized by sickness and hunger, the Confederate Army surrendered Vicksburg on July 4—just a day after General Robert E. Lee was defeated at Gettysburg, signaling a sea change in the war.

❶ Don't miss this! Would you like someone to ride along in your car and explain the siege to you in detail as you complete the 16-mile driving tour? Vicksburg National Military Park can supply you with a licensed park guide who can not only tell you everything you want to know about the military operations, but who is equally familiar with the rigors of civilian life during the months of battle. The whole tour takes about two hours, with time for whatever stops you'd like to make along the way at monuments, the USS *Cairo* Museum, or any of the battlefield overlooks. To be sure there's a guide for you on the day you'd like to tour, reserve one in advance by calling the visitor center at 601–636–0583 or 601–636–3827.

Hours: The USS *Cairo* Museum is open October to March from 8:30 A.M. to 5:00 P.M., and March to October from 9:30 A.M. to 6:00 P.M. It is closed Thanksgiving, Christmas, and New Year's Day.

The Vicksburg Visitor Center is open daily from 8:00 A.M. to 5:00 P.M. It is closed Thanksgiving, Christmas, and New Year's Day.

Fees: Admission is $8.00 per vehicle.

How to get there: To reach the park from the east or west, take Interstate 20 to Vicksburg. Take exit 4B, and follow Clay Street (U.S. Highway 80) west 0.25 mile to the park entrance.

From the north, take Interstate 55 south to Jackson. To save time, you can use the Interstate 220 bypass on the west side of Jackson to reach I–20. Take I–20 west to Vicksburg and exit 4B, approximately 40 miles, then follow the directions above to the site.

From the south, take I–55 or U.S. Highway 49 to Jackson. Take I–20 west to Vicksburg exit 4B, approximately 42 miles, then follow the directions above to the site at 3201 Clay Street in Vicksburg.

Stamping Locations and What the Cancellations Say

Main Park visitor center
3201 Clay Street
(601) 636–0583
☐ Vicksburg Nat'l Military Park/Vicksburg, MS ⓿

USS *Cairo* Museum
(601) 636–2199
Located at mile 7.8 on the park tour road
☐ U.S.S. Cairo Museum/Vicksburg, MS ⓿

North Carolina

39 Blue Ridge Parkway

Headquarters in Asheville, North Carolina
(828) 298–0398
www.nps.gov/blri
Eastern time zone

Number of cancellations: Ten, plus a cancellation for the Overmountain Victory Trail, one for Great Smoky Mountains National Park, and one for the Blue Ridge National Heritage Area. More parkway cancellations are available in Virginia.

Difficulty: Challenging

About this site: The single most visited national park unit, the Blue Ridge Parkway winds for 469 miles through the southern Appalachian Mountains, from Waynesboro, Virginia, to Cherokee, North Carolina. In between, the parkway presents some of the most delightfully peaceful blue-green expanses of mountains, hillside, farmland, and forest this side of the Mississippi River.

With its characteristic bluish haze—caused by hydrocarbons released into the air by the millions of trees and other vegetation that thrive in the temperate climate—the Blue Ridge itself actually extends from northern Georgia into Pennsylvania. The parkway extends through the Blude Ridge, Black, Great Craggy, Great Balsam, and Plott Balsam Mountains. Its final miles meander through the Great Smoky Mountains.

Stamping tips: Only four of the cancellation stamp stops on the parkway in North Carolina are open year-round: the Folk Art Center, the Destination Center, the Museum of North Carolina Minerals, and the Oconaluftee Visitor Center in Great Smoky Mountains National Park. To make the end-to-end drive and get all the cancellations in one go, travel between Memorial Day and mid-fall, as even the centers that open in April and May often keep limited hours or are closed for several days each week.

If you're making the end-to-end drive, including Virginia, plan to spend at least two days and possibly three on the road. With the reduced speed limit, the wealth of scenic and cultural sites to explore, and the opportunities for hiking, biking, picnicking, and shopping off the beaten path, rushing through the Blue Ridge is almost sacrilegious. Additional cancellations are available in Virginia.

Don't miss this! Where there's stunning scenery, there are also usually luxury homes—and the mansion of Moses H. Cone proves this rule. A sprawling, twenty-three room country home the textile magnate built on 3,600 acres of land, Flat Top Manor now holds the Parkway craft center, a terrific place to find special gifts made by the artists of the Southern Appalachian region. Carriage roads built by Cone remain open and well groomed for hikers, horseback riders, and joggers.

How the Linville Gorge, the Linville Falls Fault, and the area mountain ranges came to offer so many natural resources through the mining of minerals and gemstones is the question explored in depth at the Museum of North Carolina Minerals. A major renovation and expansion in 2002 provided interactive exhibits and detailed displays on the not-so-mysterious continental movements that produced the wealth of raw materials below the surface.

If you feel like you haven't had a good, powerful walk yet on the parkway, Waterrock Knob will do the trick. This steep, 0.5-mile (each way) trail ascends to the highest walkable elevation on the parkway—some 6,400 feet. Your lungs will feel the altitude change if you're not already acclimated, but the view from the summit provides the exertion-justifying payoff, even on a cloudy or misty day. Not up for the climb? Take in the satisfying views from the parking lot. You don't even have to leave your car to see what makes this parkway pulloff so popular.

Hours: All seasonal opening and closing dates are approximate and may change based on weather and staffing.

Moses H. Cone Visitor Center is open from early May to Memorial Day, Wednesday to Sunday from 9:00 A.M. to 5:00 P.M., and closed Monday and Tuesday. From Memorial Day to early November, it is open daily from 9:00 A.M. to 5:00 P.M. It is closed from early November to early May.

Linn Cove Viaduct Visitor Center is open daily, from the end of April to late October, from 9:00 A.M. to 5:00 P.M. It is closed from early November to the end of April.

Linville Falls Visitor Center is open from April 1 to late April on Saturday and Sunday only, from 9:00 A.M. to 5:00 P.M. From late April to late May, it is open Thursday to Monday from 9:00 A.M. to 5:00 P.M., and closed Tuesday and Wednesday. From late May to early November, it is open daily from 9:00 A.M. to 5:00 P.M. It is closed from early November to early April.

Museum of North Carolina Minerals is open daily year-round, from 9:00 A.M. to 5:00 P.M.

Craggy Gardens Visitor Center is open on weekends only the second and third weeks of April: Friday, Saturday, and Sunday from 10:00 A.M. to 4:00 P.M. From the end of April to the end of May, it is open daily from 10:00 A.M. to 4:00 P.M. From the end of May to early November it is open daily from 9:00 A.M. to 5:00 P.M. It is closed from early November to mid-April.

The **Folk Art Center** is open daily year-round. From the end of May to early November, hours are from 9:00 A.M. to 6:00 P.M. For the rest of the year, hours are from 9:00 A.M. to 5:00 P.M. It is closed Thanksgiving, Christmas, and New Year's Day.

Blue Ridge Parkway Destination Center is open dail year-round from 9:00 A.M. to 5:00 P.M. It is closed Thanksgiving, Christmas and New Year's Day.

Waterrock Knob Visitor Center is open from late April to late May, Thursday to Monday from 10:00 A.M. to 4:00 P.M.; it is closed Tuesday and Wednesday. From late May to October 31, it is open daily from 10:00 A.M. to 5:00 P.M. It is closed from November to late April.

Oconaluftee Visitor Center is open daily year-round. In May, hours are from 9:00 A.M. to 6:00 P.M. From June through August, hours are from 8:00 A.M. to 7:00 P.M. In September and October, hours are from 8:00 A.M. to 6:00 P.M. From November to April, hours are from 9:00 A.M. to 4:30 P.M.

Fees: There are no tolls or admission fees for use of the parkway. Some privately run sites may charge fees for admission.

How to get there: The motor road is marked every mile by concrete mileposts, beginning with milepost 0 near Shenandoah National Park and ending with milepost 469 at Great Smoky Mountain National Park. The winding nature of the road and change in elevation mean that those driving large recreational vehicles will have to allow for lots of extra time. Personal vehicles, motorcycles, tour buses, and bicycles are allowed.

Stamping Locations and What the Cancellations Say

Moses H. Cone Memorial Park Visitor Center
Mile 294.1
(828) 295–3782
☐ Blue Ridge Parkway/Cone Memorial Park **Ⓤ**

Linn Cove Viaduct Visitor Center
Mile 304.0
(828) 733–1354
☐ Blue Ridge Parkway/Linn Cove Viaduct **Ⓤ**

Linville Falls Visitor Center
Mile 316.4
(828) 765–1045
☐ Blue Ridge Parkway/North Carolina–Virginia **Ⓓ**
☐ Blue Ridge Parkway/Linnville Falls **Ⓤ**

Museum of North Carolina Minerals
Mile 331.0
(828) 765–2761
☐ Blue Ridge Parkway/Museum of N.C. Minerals **Ⓤ**
☐ Overmountain Victory Trail/Blue Ridge Parkway **Ⓤ**

Craggy Gardens Visitor Center
Mile 364.6
☐ Blue Ridge Parkway/Craggy Gardens **Ⓤ**

Folk Art Center
Mile 382.0
(828) 298–7928
☐ Blue Ridge Parkway/Folk Art Center **Ⓤ**

Blue Ridge Parkway Destination Center
Mile 384.0
(828) 298–5330
☐ Blue Ridge Parkway/Destination Center **Ⓤ**
☐ Blue Ridge Nat'l Heritage Area/Asheville, NC **Ⓤ**

Waterrock Knob Visitor Center
Mile 451.2
☐ Blue Ridge Parkway/Waterrock Knob ⓞ

Oconaluftee Visitor Center
Great Smoky Mountains National Park
Mile 469
(828) 497–1904
☐ Blue Ridge Parkway/North Carolina VA ⓞ
☐ Great Smoky Mts. National Park/Oconaluftee Visitor
   Center N.C. ⓞ

40 Cape Hatteras National Seashore

Manteo, North Carolina
(252) 473–2111
www.nps.gov/caha
Eastern time zone

Number of cancellations: Three

Difficulty: Tricky

About this site: It's hard to imagine, when you're standing on the beach at Cape Hatteras National Seashore on a day when the sea laps gently against the shore, that these languid barrier islands have seen more than 500 shipwrecks, German U-boat activity, and even honest-to-goodness piracy in their centuries of history.

Just off the coast of Cape Hatteras, the Atlantic turns treacherous as the warm Gulf Stream meets the colder Virginia Coastal Drift, forcing ships to veer dangerously off course and run aground on shoals as much as 10 miles beyond the shore. The lighthouses were the only dependable landmarks for wayward navigators throughout the nineteenth and twentieth centuries. Storms buffeted the towers, erosion threatened their foundations, and wars shut down their beacons, but the Cape Hatteras lighthouses endured—with reconstruction, relocation, and refortification to retain their guiding power.

Stamping tips: On the surface, you might think it's easy to get these three cancellations, as the visitor centers all are open 364 days a year. To reach Ocracoke, however, you must take a forty-minute ferry ride across the channel from Hatteras, which may slow your stamping day as you wait for the boat to depart. The good news is that this state-operated ferry is offered free as a courtesy to park visitors, and it departs every half hour from 8:00 A.M. to 8:00 P.M. during the high season (May to October), with hourly departures from 9:00 P.M. to midnight and from 5:00 A.M. to 7:00 A.M. From November to April, the ferry departs hourly from 5:00 A.M. to midnight. Visit www.ncdot.org/transit/ferry/routes/schedule/route003.html for a full ferry schedule.

Don't miss this! The secret to fully appreciating these barrier islands is in knowing where to look, and no one knows where to find the natural and cultural treasures of the cape more than the rangers who walk these paths and shores every day. Try one of the dozens of ranger-led activities offered during the summer months: Morning bird walks reveal the nesting sites of shorebird and long-legged wading species; treks from beach to woods turn up unusual, barrier island-loving plants and woodland creatures; history programs cover the Outer Banks and the solitary life of the lighthouse keeper, and even the swashbuckling days of wide-spread piracy on the high seas.

Hours: The Bodie Island Visitor Center is open daily year-round. From the second Sunday in June through Labor Day, hours are from 9:00 A.M. to 6:00 P.M., and from Labor Day through mid-June, hours are from 9:00 A.M. to 5:00 P.M. It is closed Christmas.

Hatteras Island Visitor Center is open daily year-round. From the second Sunday in June through Labor Day, hours are from 9:00 A.M. to 6:00 P.M., and from Labor Day through mid-June, hours are from 9:00 A.M. to 5:00 P.M. It is closed Christmas.

Ocracoke Visitor Center is open daily year-round. From the second Sunday in June through Labor Day, hours are from 9:00 A.M. to 6:00 P.M., and from Labor Day through mid-June, hours are from 9:00 A.M. to 5:00 P.M. It is closed Christmas.

Fees: Admission to this park is free. Fees are charged to climb Hatteras Lighthouse: $7.00 for adults, $3.50 for children and seniors sixty-two and older.

How to get there: There are three major access routes to North Carolina 12, which is the only major route through the park.

From the north, U.S. Highway 158 accesses the Outer Banks at Kitty Hawk, and then intersects NC 12 at the park's northern entrance, below Nags Head.

From the west, U.S. Highway 64/264 comes over Roanoke Island and intersects NC 12 at the park's northern entrance.

From South Carolina, take Interstate 95 to Wilson, North Carolina. Take US 264 east through Greenville and Washington, North Carolina. From Washington, take North Carolina 30 to Plymouth and the junction with US 64, and take US 64 east to Nags Head and the junction of NC 12 South.

Stamping Locations and What the Cancellations Say

Bodie Island Visitor Center
(252) 441–5711
Located on NC 12 6.5 miles south of the US 158/NC 12/US 64/264 intersection (Whalebone Junction) at Nags Head
☐ Cape Hatteras Nat'l Seashore/Nags Head, NC ⓤ

Hatteras Visitor Center
(252) 995–4474
Located at the Cape Hatteras Lighthouse in Buxton
☐ Cape Hatteras Nat'l Seashore/Buxton, NC ⓤ

Ocracoke Visitor Center
(252) 928–4531
Located in Ocracoke at the southern end of NC 12; a ferry is required to reach this island.
☐ Cape Hatteras National Seashore/Ocracoke Island, NC ⓤ

41 Cape Lookout National Seashore

Harkers Island, North Carolina
(252) 728–2250
www.nps.gov/calo
Eastern time zone

Number of cancellations: Three

Difficulty: Heroic

About this site: If the seven-year-old kid in you still wishes he or she could sail the high seas in search of treasure, then a visit to Cape Lookout is an absolute must. Here the notorious Blackbeard, the most dastardly and dangerous pirate of the 1700s, led his crew of 300 men in a spree of looting, burning, and sinking ships in and around North Carolina's coastal waters for an action-packed eighteen months, until Lieutenant Robert Maynard killed the pirate for reward money.

Stamping tips: While the Harkers Island Visitor Center is open year-round, the other two stamping sites are on islands that can only be reached by ferry (or private boat, if you have one), and they're only open April through November. To fully experience this park, you will need to visit in season—and you'll take two different ferries to reach the lighthouse and Portsmouth Village, leaving from two different points.

Ferry services to the Cape Lookout Lighthouse leave from Harkers Island or from Beaufort. You have six services from which to choose, all of which take passengers only (no vehicles), so be prepared to walk on the island.

From Harkers Island: Calico Jacks Ferry (252–728–3575); Harkers Island Fishing Center (252–728–3907); Island Ferry Adventures at Barbour's Marina (252–728–6181).

From Beaufort: Mystery Tours (252–728–7827); Outer Banks Ferry Service (252–728–4129).

Only one ferry service, run by Captain Rudy Austin, travels to Portsmouth Village. You can reach him for schedules, fare information, and reservations at 252–928–4361. The Portsmouth Village ferry leaves from Ocracoke.

Depending on your level of interest in each of the stamping stops, it's likely that you'll need to plan two days for stamping in Cape Lookout, perhaps in conjunction with your time at Cape Hatteras. On all of the ferries, make reservations at least a day or more in advance. Otherwise, you may find yourself standing in line for long periods while ferries come and go—and there's no more frustrating activity than waiting when you're on a cancellation stamp quest.

There's one more thing to keep in mind while you're visiting Portsmouth Village: This island's modest facilities are staffed entirely by two volunteers, who are often out of the hut during the day, chatting with visitors in Portsmouth Village or tending to park responsibilities on the island—or they may make trips to the mainland, especially if storms are predicted, and may have difficulty returning after a major weather event. Rangers at Cape Lookout say collecting the cancellation on Portsmouth Island is hit-or-miss at best, so check at the Harkers Island Visitor Center before making the trip out to Portsmouth, just in case the rangers know the cancellation won't be available.

❶ Don't miss this! This is the place to get away from it all—three sandy islands with no roads or developed areas, and no groomed trails for hikers or bikers. Leave your car on the mainland and be prepared to walk in soft sand.

Shell collecting is not only allowed, it's encouraged—in fact, you can take two gallons' worth of empty shells away from the park with you (leave creature-filled shells where you find them). You'll be well rewarded for your trip to Portsmouth Village, a ghost town once inhabited by people who worked as "lighterers." This specialized profession served large ships that made use of the access provided by Ocracoke Inlet from the Atlantic Ocean to Pamlico Sound and the mainland. The inlet's shallow water proved treacherous for heavily laden ships, so the people of Portsmouth would unload cargo on the ocean side into small flat-boats, allow the ships to pass through the inlet, and reload them when the ships reached deeper water. This highly localized activity earned Portsmouth residents a good living until 1846, when a hurricane opened Hatteras Inlet as a deeper and more desirable route than Ocracoke. Many people abandoned Portsmouth during the Civil War; the rest trickled away as better opportunities arose elsewhere.

A tip from the rangers: Wear your most effective insect repellent, and carry it with you for additional applications. Mosquitoes here are hungry and fierce!

Hours: Harkers Island Visitor Center is open daily year-round, from 9:00 A.M. to 5:00 P.M. It is closed Christmas and New Year's Day.

Cape Lookout Lighthouse Keepers Quarters is open from April 1 to the day after Thanksgiving, from 9:00 A.M. to 5:00 P.M. It is closed from the end of November through March 31.

Portsmouth Village is open April through November, from 9:00 A.M. to 5:00 P.M.

Fees: Admission to the park is free. All ferry services have fees for passage to the islands; check the ferries' Web site at www.nps.gov/calo/planyourvisit/ferry.htm for schedule and prices.

How to get there: Cape Lookout National Seashore's visitor center is located on the eastern end of Harkers Island, about 20 miles east of Beaufort.

From Beaufort, take U.S. 70 east to Harkers Island Road (North Carolina 1332/1335).

From Cedar Island, take North Carolina 12 south past the Atlantic turnoff to US 70 west. Continue on US 70 to Harkers Island Road (NC 1332/1335). Follow Harkers Island Road to its end. The visitor center is on the left.

Stamping Locations and What the Cancellations Say

Harkers Island Visitor Center
(252) 728–2250
Located on the east end of Harkers Island at the end of Harkers Island Road

☐ Cape Lookout National Seashore/Harkers Island, NC ⓞ

Cape Lookout Lighthouse Keepers' Quarters
No phone; call 252–728–2250 for information
Located on South Core Banks near Bardens Inlet. This area is reachable only by private boat or passenger ferries.

☐ Cape Lookout National Seashore/Keepers' Quarters, NC ⓞ

Portsmouth Village Visitor Center
No phone; call 252–728–2250 for information
Located on Portsmouth Island, reachable only by ferry from Ocracoke

☐ Cape Lookout National Seashore/Portsmouth Village, NC ⓞ

42 Carl Sandburg Home National Historic Site

Flat Rock, North Carolina
(828) 693–4178
www.nps.gov/carl
Eastern time zone

Number of cancellations: One
Difficulty: Easy

About this site: He won a Pulitzer Prize for history in 1940 for his four-volume biography, *Abraham Lincoln: The War Years,* and won the Pulitzer again in 1951 for his *Complete Poems,* a compilation of his life's work in verse up to that point. Carl Sandburg earned his fame as a poet, novelist, children's author, journalist, biographer, social activist, and historian, all of which are celebrated at Connemara, the last home he shared with his wife, Lilian Steichen Sandburg.

Born in a modest home in Galesburg, Illinois, and working in obscurity until he was thirty-six years old, Sandburg spent years as a journalist for the *Chicago Daily News* until 1914, when a group of his poems in *Poetry* magazine demonstrated his genius with the written word. Two years later, his first anthology, *Chicago Poems,* made him one of America's most original and beloved poets.

❶ Don't miss this! Lilian Sandburg raised prize-winning dairy goats in the barn that now houses fine specimens of each of her three most valued breeds. You can meet these beautiful animals and learn about them from rangers at the historic barn, from which Mrs. Sandburg ran her dairy goat operation. Your visit to the barn is free.

Hours: The site is open daily year-round, from 9:00 A.M. to 5:00 P.M. It is closed Christmas.

Fees: Admission is $5.00 for adults for the tour, $3.00 for seniors sixty-two and older, and free for children sixteen and younger.

How to get there: The park is 3 miles south of Hendersonville, off the Greenville Highway/North Carolina 225. From Interstate 26, take exit 53. Turn right onto Upward Road if traveling east; turn left onto Upward Road if traveling west. At the intersection with Spartanburg Highway, continue straight; Upward Road becomes North Highland Lake Road. At the light, turn left onto NC 225/Greenville Highway south. At the next light, take a right onto Little River Road. Visitor parking is on the left.

Stamping Locations and What the Cancellations Say
Visitor center on the first level of the home

☐ Carl Sandburg Home NHS/Flat Rock, NC ❶

43 Fort Raleigh National Historic Site

Manteo, North Carolina
(252) 473–5772
www.nps.gov/fora
Eastern time zone

Number of cancellations: Two, plus one for the Underground Railroad

Difficulty: Easy

About this site: It's one of the greatest unsolved mysteries in American history: An entire colony of 116 English citizens settled at Fort Raleigh in 1585, years before John Smith's 1607 arrival at Jamestown... but the ill-fated settlers of Fort Raleigh disappeared, leaving not a trace of evidence to hint at the cause of their demise.

Uneasy relations with the local Indian tribe, misdirected attempts to bring new supplies to the colony from England, desertion by an early group of settlers, and a host of other challenges made for a tough life at Fort Raleigh even in the best of circumstances. When colony governor John White returned to Fort Raleigh after an extended trip back to England, he found no sign of the colonists—not even graves—except for the three letters "CRO" carved into a tree. To this day, scientists have found no conclusive evidence to suggest the end met by colonists at the tip of Roanoke Island.

❶ Don't miss this! Your experience at Fort Raleigh just won't be complete unless you attend a performance of *The Lost Colony,* one of the longest running outdoor dramas in the country. It's written by Pulitzer Prize-winning playwright Paul Green and performed in the historic Waterside Theatre on Roanoke Island, and it's an educational and entertaining event the whole family will enjoy. For tickets and show times, visit www.thelostcolony.org.

Hours: The site is open daily year-round, from 9:00 A.M. to 5:00 P.M. It is closed Christmas. During the summer when *The Lost Colony* outdoor drama is presented, the visitor center is open until 6:00 P.M.

Fees: Admission to the park is free.

How to get there: The park is 3 miles north of Manteo. From the north via Norfolk, Virginia, take Interstate 64E south to Virginia 168 (this becomes North Carolina 168 at the state line), or take

U.S. Highway 17 south. Follow either highway to U.S. Highway 158. Continue south on US 158 onto the Outer Banks, where the highway merges with North Carolina 12. Continue south to Whalebone. Turn west on US 158 at Whalebone, and cross Roanoke Sound onto Roanoke Island. Here US 158 joins U.S. Highways 264/64. Continue on US 264/64 to Fort Raleigh.

From the west, take US 64 east from Raleigh to Roanoke Island.

From the south, take Interstate 95 to Rocky Mount, where you can pick up US 64. Follow US 64 east to the site.

Stamping Locations and What the Cancellations Say
Visitor center bookstore
(252) 473–5582

☐ Ft. Raleigh Nat'l Hist Site/Manteo, NC ⓾

☐ Ft. Raleigh NHS/Roanoke Island, NC ⓾

☐ Ft. Raleigh NHS/Underground RR Freedom Network ⓾

▐44▐ Great Smoky Mountains National Park

Cherokee, North Carolina
(865) 436–1200
www.nps.gov/grsm
Eastern time zone

Number of cancellations: Two: one for the park, plus a cancellation for the Blue Ridge Parkway. More cancellations for this park are available in Tennessee.

Difficulty: Easy

About this site: From the diversity of wildlife—12,000 documented species of plants, trees, mammals, birds, fish, reptiles, amphibians, and insects, with speculation that there may be tens of thousands more—to the wild southern Appalachian mountain range, the Great Smoky Mountains deliver on their promise of a rich, meticulously preserved biosphere snatched back from the brink of overdevelopment. This is the most visited of all of America's national parks, and its spectacular views and abundant opportunities for outdoor recreation make it clear why more than nine million people flock to the park every year.

❶ Don't miss this! Several hiking trails begin at or near the Oconaluftee Visitor Center and traverse this pastoral corner of North Carolina—for a map with full details of the park's 850 miles of trails, visit www.nps.gov/grsm/pphtml/maps.html.

Adjacent to the Oconaluftee Visitor Center, you'll find the Mountain Farm Museum, a collection of historic buildings from many locations in the park. The Davis Queen House, built of American chestnut, is one of the last homes constructed from these trees before the chestnut blight of the 1930s and 1940s killed off the species and made the wood a very high-priced item.

Hours: Oconaluftee Visitor Center is open daily year-round. In May, hours are from 8:30 A.M. to 5:00 P.M. From June through August, hours are from 8:00 A.M. to 6:00 P.M. In September and October, hours are from 8:30 A.M. to 5:00 P.M. From November through April, hours are from 8:30 A.M. to 4:30 P.M. The center is closed Christmas.

Fees: Admission to the park is free.

How to get there: To reach the Cherokee entrance to the park from Interstate 40, take U.S. Highway 19 West through Maggie Valley. Proceed to U.S. Highway 441 at Cherokee, and follow US 441 north into the park.

From Atlanta, Georgia, and points south, follow US 441 and U.S. Highway 23 north; US 441 leads to Cherokee and the park entrance.

Stamping Locations and What the Cancellations Say

Oconaluftee Visitor Center
(828) 497–1904
Located inside the park, 2 miles north of Cherokee, on US 441

☐ Great Smoky Mts. National Park/Oconaluftee Visitor Center N.C. ❶

☐ Blue Ridge Parkway/North Carolina VA ❶

45 Guilford Courthouse National Military Park

Greensboro, North Carolina
(336) 288–1776
www.nps.gov/guco
Eastern time zone

Number of cancellations: One

Difficulty: Easy

About this site: The battle that took place here on March 15, 1781, pitted 4,500 militia and Continental troops, a critical arm of the Continental Army, against far fewer—but far more experienced—British forces in one of the most dramatic events of the American Revolution. As Major General Nathanael Greene faced Lord Charles Cornwallis and his army of British regulars and German allies, Greene discovered that his own troops—more than twice as many as the redcoats and their allies combined—could not best the more seasoned veterans, and he was forced to leave the field of battle. While Greene could not declare the day an American victory, his efforts set up the British commander for defeat and surrender at Yorktown seven months later.

❶ Don't miss this! You have many options for exploring this battlefield. You can buy the compact disc and take the two-hour driving tour; you can take your bike and ride the 2.25-mile loop; or you can walk the trails and the historic New Garden Road to absorb the troop maneuvers at a slower pace. If your time is short, watch the excellent film, *Another Such Victory,* shown in the visitor center.

Hours: The park is open daily year-round, from 8:30 A.M. to 5:00 P.M. It is closed New Year's Day, Thanksgiving, and Christmas.

Fees: Admission to the park is free.

How to get there: From Interstate 85 southbound approaching Greensboro, take Business I–85/Interstate 40, and then exit onto U.S. Highway 840 (exit 131). Go north 2 miles, and exit on U.S. Highway 70 westbound (Burlington Road). Continue west toward Greensboro, and exit on Ohenry Boulevard. Continue north on Ohenry for 2 miles, and exit on West Cone Boulevard. Go west 5 miles to Battleground Avenue, and turn right onto U.S. Highway 220 northbound. Go 3 miles north to New Garden Road; turn right, and continue to the park at 2332 New Garden Road.

From I–85 northbound approaching Greensboro, take Business I–85. Exit on Holden Road (exit 34). Turn right, and go north 6 miles, crossing Bryan Boulevard to Benjamin Parkway. Turn left on Benjamin Parkway. Go one block, and turn left on Battleground Avenue, then follow the directions given above.

From I–40 eastbound, as you enter Greensboro, exit on Guilford College/Jamestown Road (exit 213). Turn right on Guilford College Road after crossing the interstate bridge. Go north 2 miles. Continue north past the Guilford College campus, and turn right on New Garden Road. Go east 3 miles, crossing Battleground Avenue, to the park.

Stamping Locations and What the Cancellations Say
Guilford Courthouse Visitor Center front desk

☐ Guilford Courthouse National Military Park/Greensboro, NC ⓤ

46 Moores Creek National Battlefield

Currie, North Carolina
(910) 283–5591
www.nps.gov/mocr
Eastern time zone

Number of cancellations: One

Difficulty: Easy

About this site: In the skirmishes that preceded the signing of the Declaration of Independence, Americans proved to their British loyalist foes that might did not necessarily equal right, and that passion could triumph over boldness. On February 27, 1776, Scottish settlers and Carolina loyalists tramped across the Moores Creek bridge in a mighty charge, believing that the American militia was retreating and the day was already won. When nearly a thousand militia suddenly fired muskets and cannons from well-concealed posts, they felled the loyalist commanders and scattered the troops in a panic that belied their earlier bluster. The surviving loyalists retreated en masse, leaving behind weapons, ammunition, and supplies worth their weight in gold to the American forces. Two months later, North Carolina became the first colony to vote in favor of independence.

❶ Don't miss this! Walk to the historic bridge site by taking the 1-mile interpretive trail, which provides wayside exhibits that explain troop movements and the critical events of the brief but important battle. You'll walk in the footsteps of the loyalists who expected an easy evening's passage and found a raging hive of firepower, and you'll see the grounds on which the Americans concealed themselves and their weapons until the right moment, and then rained musket and cannon fire on their foes.

Hours: The battlefield is open daily year-round, from 9:00 A.M. to 5:00 P.M. It is closed Thanksgiving, Christmas, and New Year's Day.

Fees: Admission to the park is free.

How to get there: The park is located at 40 Patriots Hall Drive in Currie, on North Carolina 210, about 3 miles west of U.S. Highway 421. The park also is accessible from Interstate 40 by taking NC 210 west about 15 miles to the park.

Stamping Locations and What the Cancellations Say
Moores Creek Visitor Center

☐ Moores Creek Nat'l Battlefield/Currie, NC ❶

47 Wright Brothers National Memorial

Manteo, North Carolina
(252) 441–7430
www.nps.gov/wrbr
Eastern time zone
Number of cancellations: One
Difficulty: Easy
About this site: If ever there was a monument to ingenuity, tenacity, perseverance, and sheer human drive, the Wright Brothers Memorial at Kill Devil Hills is it—a 60-foot granite edifice that reminds us of December 17, 1903, when the Wright brothers, bicycle shop owners from Dayton, Ohio, saw the culmination of four years of experiments, failures, redesigns, and reattempts by making the first-ever manned air flight. Drawing on the world's collective understanding of aeronautics and finding solutions for obstacles that had baffled others for centuries, Wilbur and

Orville Wright made four successful flights that day on these lands outside of Kitty Hawk—the longest clocking in at 59 seconds and 852 feet, with Wilbur at the helm of the Wright brothers' powered glider.

❶ Don't miss this! The 1902 glider and the 1903 Wright Flyer displayed in the visitor center are replicas, but that doesn't diminish the awesome power of seeing these flimsy, rudimentary flying machines and realizing just what the Wright brothers accomplished by getting one of them off the ground and into the air.

To feel the full impact of Wilber and Orville's achievement, spend time at the visitor center and listen to a ranger describe that day in 1903 when the Wright Flyer left the ground and carried Orville for 120 feet in twelve seconds, suddenly making it possible for men to fly. If two bicycle mechanics from Dayton could accomplish this feat and change the course of human transportation forever, what, with our technology and access to information, could any of us accomplish today? Let this amazing place and its larger-than-life tale inspire you to take on your next challenge, whatever it might be.

Hours: The visitor center is open daily year-round. From Labor Day to Memorial Day, hours are from 9:00 A.M. to 5:00 P.M. From Memorial Day to Labor Day, hours are from 9:00 A.M. to 6:00 P.M. It is closed Christmas.

Fees: Admission is $4.00 for adults, and free to children fifteen and under.

How to get there: The park is located on the Outer Banks of North Carolina in the town of Kill Devil Hills. The visitor center is 15 miles northeast of Manteo on U.S. Highway 158, at 1401 National Park Drive.

Stamping Locations and What the Cancellations Say

Visitor center

☐ Wright Brothers Nat'l Memorial/Kill Devil Hills, NC ❶

Puerto Rico

48 San Juan National Historic Site

San Juan, Puerto Rico
(787) 729–6777
www.nps.gov/saju
Atlantic time zone

Number of cancellations: Seven

Difficulty: Easy

About this site: When explorers arrived in the New World and claimed the Caribbean islands for Spain, the proclamation invited nearly constant challenges from pirates, native adversaries, and European invaders who wanted their share of the area's riches. King Philip II of Spain responded by ordering the building of two forts that still stand in old San Juan, the colonists' first defense against English and Dutch interlopers. Today these are the oldest remaining fortifications constructed by Spain in America.

Stamping tips: Chances are that if you're planning to visit this site, you've booked passage on a cruise ship and have limited time in San Juan to secure your cancellations and still enjoy this captivating island. If you've flown into San Juan, you may have more time to explore—but either way, the good news is that while there are seven cancellations here in two different buildings, you'll have no trouble collecting them all in one visit. Note that some of the nearly identical cancellations have slight differences in punctuation.

Don't miss this! This historic site received a special honor in 1983: It became one of only twenty properties in the United States that are designated World Heritage Sites by the United Nations Educational, Scientific, and Cultural Organization (UNESCO). This places San Juan National Historic Site among the ranks of the Great Wall of China, the Taj Mahal, the Old City of Jerusalem, and the Volcanoes of Kamchatka in its significance to world history. Take the ranger-guided tour of the fortifications and see what it took for Spain to hold onto this island in the face of one invasion force after another—and why these forts are still standing centuries after their construction, despite winds, salt spray, tropical storms, and military bombardment.

Hours: The site is open daily year-round. From June to November, hours are from 9:00 A.M. to 5:00 P.M. From December to May, hours are from 9:00 A.M. to 6:00 P.M.

Fees: Admission is $3.00 for adults if visiting only one fortification, and $5.00 for both. Children fifteen and under are admitted free.

How to get there: If you are arriving in Puerto Rico on a cruise ship, most piers are within walking distance (ten to fifteen minutes). Just walk up the hill, past the Plaza Colon. The Panamerican pier is 3 miles away, and taxis are available.

Stamping Locations and What the Cancellations Say

San Felipe del Morro entrance
(787) 729–6777

☐ SAN JUAN NATIONAL HISTORIC SITE/
OLD SAN JUAN, P. R. **Ⓤ**

San Felipe del Morro Gift Shop
(787) 725–4009

☐ San Juan National Historic Site/Old San Juan, PR **Ⓓ**

San Antonio Guard House Gift Shop
(787) 729–6754 ext. 27

☐ San Juan National Historic Site/Old San Juan, PR **Ⓓ**

San Cristobal
Visitor center entrance
(787) 729–6777

☐ Old San Juan National Historic Site/San Cristobal **Ⓓ**

San Cristobal
Main plaza entrance
(787) 729–6777

☐ San Juan National Historic Site/Old San Juan, PR Ⓓ

San Cristobal
Visitor center gift shop, next to the entrance
(787) 729–6777

☐ Old San Juan National Historic Site/San Cristobal Ⓓ

San Cristobal
Gift shop on the main plaza
(787) 724–1260

☐ San Juan National Historic Site/Old San Juan PR Ⓓ

South Carolina

49 Charles Pinckney National Historic Site

Mount Pleasant, South Carolina
(843) 881–5516
www.nps.gov/chpi
Eastern time zone

Number of cancellations: One

Difficulty: Easy

About this site: Charles Pinckney's name may not be a household word, but his influence on the development of the United States Constitution won him a lasting place in history. A patriot who was imprisoned by the British for nearly a year during the Revolution, Pinckney emerged after the war as an enlightened leader whom South Carolina quickly chose to represent the state in Congress. History credits him with constitutional clauses including the House of Representatives' right to choose its own Speaker of the House; congressional regulation of foreign trade; and the law banning religious discrimination against a candidate for public office. Once the Constitution was ratified, Pinckney went on to become an ambassador, facilitating the transfer of the Louisiana Territory from France to the United States.

Don't miss this! Snee Farm belonged to the Pinckney family until Charles Pinckey sold it in 1817, but the house you see today did not belong to the Pinckneys. In fact, the artifacts that relate to Pinckney's day have all been discovered on this site since 1987, when archeological excavation began, and scientists and historians now believe that the house was built in 1828, after hurricanes destroyed the Pinckney property.

Most interesting, however, is the wealth of information unearthed in the last two decades about the slave population on the one-time 715-acre plantation (now twenty-eight acres), and about their labors and living conditions. You'll find an overview of the archeologists' findings at the visitor center inside the house.

Hours: The site is open daily year-round, from 9:00 A.M. to 5:00 P.M. It is closed New Year's Day, Thanksgiving, and Christmas.

Fees: Admission to the park is free.

How to get there: The site is 6 miles north of Charleston and can be reached via U.S. Highway 17 north in Mount Pleasant. Turn left on Long Point Road, and travel 0.5 mile. The site entrance is on the left, at 1254 Long Point Road in Mount Pleasant.

From Interstate 526, exit at Long Point Road, turn left at the light, and travel 3 miles. The site entrance is on the right.

Stamping Locations and What the Cancellations Say
Inside main house

☐ Charles Pinckney NHS/Mt. Pleasant, SC ❶

50 Congaree National Park

Hopkins, South Carolina
(803) 776–4396
www.nps.gov/cosw
Eastern time zone

Number of cancellations: One

Difficulty: Easy

About this site: If you've never had the chance to see old-growth forest, you'll find more than 22,000 acres of the largest, oldest trees this side of the Mississippi River at Congaree National Park—tall, neck-cracking hardwoods that have thrived for centuries in this constantly sultry floodplain, a richly fertile swath of bottomland cut with creeks and streams that nourish the swamp's lacework of tree roots. The result is a tranquil, sumptuously green sanctuary open for exploration by water or land.

❶ **Don't miss this!** Lots of easy to moderate trails take you deep into the forest, where you'll see Tolkien-like cypress root "knees" protruding from the forest floor and peacefully burbling streams crisscrossing the paths. Choose a boardwalk stroll with elevated sections that allow you to look down into the swamp areas, or a longer hike past the enormous oak trees and into prime habitat for possum, river otter, deer, or even a bobcat. Birders should check at the visitor center for recent sightings of the Swainson's warbler or red-cockaded woodpecker, one of the rarest of Congaree's sought-after species. And if insects and spiders are your passion, Congaree has an embarrassment of riches—from walking sticks and pleasing fungus beetles to long-jawed orb weavers and three kinds of millipede. Oh, and mosquitoes—plenty of them. Strong, effective insect repellent is not just about minimizing an annoyance, it's about maximizing your enjoyment of this truly lovely park.

Hours: The park is open daily year-round, from 8:30 A.M. to 5:00 P.M. It is closed Christmas.

Fees: Admission to this park is free.

How to get there: From Interstate 77 near Columbia, take exit 5. Turn onto South Carolina 48 east (Bluff Road). Continue for 14 miles toward Gadsden, and turn right onto Mountain View Road. Turn right onto Old Bluff Road, and continue to the park entrance. The visitor center is at 100 National Park Road.

Stamping Locations and What the Cancellations Say

Harry Hampton Visitor Center

☐ CONGAREE NATIONAL PARK/HOPKINS, S.C. ①

51 Cowpens National Battlefield

Chesnee, South Carolina
(864) 461–2828
www.nps.gov/cowp
Eastern time zone

Number of cancellations: One for the park, and one for the Overmountain Victory Trail

Difficulty: Easy

About this site: The American Revolution took a decided turn toward patriot victory on January 17, 1781. Using a maneuver now known as double envelopment, Brigadier General Daniel Morgan of the Continental army organized three separate militias, one of Continental regulars and two of local patriots, to surround British Lieutenant Banastre Tarleton's forces at the "Cow Pens," a well-known local landmark. Morgan's tactical genius was his use of the militias, firing and then retreating behind Continental lines, leading Tarleton to expect an easy victory. Tarleton charged in without considering that Morgan knew the terrain, and suddenly found his forces surrounded by patriot troops that pinched off any hope of retreat. The resounding defeat of the British became a pivotal rallying point for the patriots.

❶ Don't miss this! To fully appreciate the strength of Morgan's strategy, view the thirteen-minute fiber-optic map presentation in the visitor center before you walk or drive the 3.8-mile auto loop, or walk the 1.2-mile interpretive trail.

Hours: The visitor center is open daily year-round, from 9:00 A.M. to 5:00 P.M. The auto loop road and picnic area close at 4:30 P.M. The battlefield is closed Thanksgiving, Christmas, and New Year's Day.

Fees: Admission to the park is free.

How to get there: From Interstate 85 north of Spartanburg, take exit 83. Turn left on South Carolina 110. Drive 8 miles. Turn right on South Carolina 11. The park entrance is about 0.5 mile on the right.

From I–85 southbound, take exit 92 at Gaffney, and head west toward Chesnee on SC 11. The park is about 10 miles down the road on the left.

From Interstate 26 eastbound, take exit 5, and go east toward Chesnee on SC 11. The park is about 20 miles distant on the right.

From I–26 westbound, take I–85 north to exit 83, and follow the directions given above.

Stamping Locations and What the Cancellations Say
Cowpens National Battlefield Visitor Center

☐ Cowpens National Battlefield/Chesnee, SC **❶**

☐ Overmountain Victory Trail/Cowpens NB **❶**

52 Fort Sumter National Monument

(including Fort Moultrie National Monument)
Sullivans Island, South Carolina
(843) 883–3123
www.nps.gov/fosu
Eastern time zone

Number of cancellations: Four

Difficulty: Tricky

About this site: Any tour of the National Park Service's many Civil War sites must include a stop at Fort Sumter, where the war saw its first battle on April 12, 1861. Four months before, South Carolina seceded from the United States. But the state's departure from the Union did not give it ownership of the federally held Fort Sumter. The fort became a Union bastion under the command of Major Robert Anderson, and with Confederate troops at nearby Fort Moultrie and Fort Johnson, Sumter held precarious ground on Charleston Harbor. At 4:30 A.M. on April 12, a mortar boomed from Fort Johnson and a 10-inch shell burst over Fort Sumter… and four years of civil war began.

When it endured its first attack in 1776, the unnamed fort across the harbor from Fort Sumter's future site was still under construction. Yet patriot forces led by Colonel William Moultrie beat back a British advance, an early triumph for the South Carolina militia. The original Fort Moultrie succumbed to years of neglect after the Revolutionary War; what you see today is the third Fort Moultrie, constructed in 1809 and in use until 1947.

Stamping tips: None of the cancellations are difficult to get, but if you want the duplicate, you must reach Fort Sumter and its accompanying museum shop by ferry. The fully narrated ferry ride is offered by Fort Sumter Tours, Inc., and the entire excursion lasts about two-and-a-quarter hours from point to point, including an hour at Fort Sumter. The ferries depart three times daily from March 1 through November 30, and twice daily in winter (except December 26 to 31, when they run three times daily). Visit www.fortsumtertours.com for the full schedule, current fees, and other ferry information, or call Fort Sumter Tours at 843–881–7337.

Don't miss this! Plan to spend some time at the visitor center at Liberty Square, where you'll find extensive information on the complex events leading up to the first shot of the Civil War. You may need an hour or more at the center before your ferry departs, depending on your level of interest in the war, but all visitors will find enlightenment here, as you learn that the war had as much to do with states' rights, sovereignty, and money as it did with the ideals of freedom and equality.

Hours and fees: Fort Sumter Visitor Education Center at Liberty Square is open daily year-round, from 8:30 A.M. to 5:00 P.M. It is closed Thanksgiving, Christmas, and New Year's Day.

Fort Sumter is open daily year-round. From March 1 to March 30, hours are from 10:00 A.M. to 4:00 P.M. From April 1 to Labor Day, hours are from 10:00 A.M. to 5:30 P.M. From the day after Labor Day to November 30, hours are from 10:00 A.M. to 4:00 P.M. From December 1 to February 28 (except the week of Christmas), hours are from 11:30 A.M. to 4:00 P.M. From December 26 to December 31, hours are from 10:00 A.M. to 4:00 P.M. The site is closed Thanksgiving, Christmas, and New Year's Day. Ferry tickets are $14.00 for adults, $8.00 for children six to eleven, $12.50 for seniors, and free for children five and under.

Fort Moultrie is open daily year-round, from 9:00 A.M. to 5:00 P.M. It is closed New Year's Day, Thanksgiving, and Christmas. Admission is $3.00 for adults, or a maximum of $5.00 per family.

How to get there: Fort Sumter is located 3.3 miles via water from downtown Charleston and must be reached by boat. You may access the Fort Sumter dock with your private boat or ride the park's concession-operated ferry system. Fort Sumter Tours, Inc., is the current authorized concession operator. The ferry departs from the visitor education center at Liberty Square (directions below).

To reach the Fort Sumter Visitor Education Center at Liberty Square from Interstate 95, take Interstate 26 east into Charleston. Exit at Meeting Street, and follow the signs to Fort Sumter and the aquarium. Pass the Charleston visitor center on the right. Proceed through the light at John and Meeting Streets. Turn left at the next light onto Calhoun Street. Proceed down Calhoun Street, passing East Bay Street and Washington Street. The parking garage for the education center is on Calhoun Street between

Washington and Concord Streets. Turn left into the garage from Calhoun Street.

To reach Fort Moultrie, take U.S. Highway 17 north from Charleston to Mount Pleasant, and bear right onto South Carolina 703. At Sullivans Island, turn right onto Middle Street. The fort and visitor center are 1.5 miles from the intersection.

Stamping Locations and What the Cancellations Say

Fort Sumter Visitor Education Center at Liberty Square
340 Concord Street
(843) 577-0242

☐ Fort Sumter National Monument/Charleston Harbor, SC **D**

☐ Liberty Square/Charleston, SC **U**

Fort Sumter Bookstore
At the fort

☐ Fort Sumter National Monument/Charleston Harbor, SC **D**

Fort Moultrie visitor center
(843) 883-3123

☐ Fort Moultrie/Sullivans Island, SC **U**

53 Historic Camden Revolutionary War Site

South Carolina NPS Affiliated Site
Camden, South Carolina
(803) 432-9841
www.historic-camden.net
Eastern time zone

Number of cancellations: One

Difficulty: Easy

About this site: After Charleston fell to the British in 1780, Lord Charles Cornwallis and 2,500 British troops marched directly to Camden, where they set up headquarters and established a major supply post for all redcoat operations in the southern colonies. Cornwallis moved into the Joseph Kershaw mansion, home of a British national who had prospered in business in

Camden, and for eleven months the colonial town suffered at the hands of the loyalists. Nearby, the Americans felt their most crushing defeat at the Battle of Camden, and then lost again to the British nearly a year later—but not before inflicting so many British casualties that the redcoats evacuated Camden.

Stamping tips: You can get this cancellation on any day of the week at the gift shop/ticket office (note the later opening time on Sunday). It's kept in a drawer, so you'll need to ask for it. But the staff is very familiar with the Passport program and will happily bring it out for you. If you take the self-guided tour, you won't be charged admission.

Don't miss this! There's a lot to see in this 107-acre outdoor museum complex, so be sure to allow a few hours to explore. Several homes have been restored to eighteenth- or nineteenth-century authenticity, including the Kershaw mansion, where Cornwallis spent a difficult year, and the John Craven House, built in 1785. If you're ready for a nice long walk, the Old Camden Trace—a 3.5-mile trail through Camden's historic district—gives you an opportunity to see how history and modern times have come together in this charming town, with its antebellum homes, centuries-old cemeteries, and fun shopping district.

Hours: On Monday, the lower grounds and shop only are open from 10:00 A.M. to 5:00 P.M. The entire site is open Tuesday through Saturday from 10:00 A.M. to 5:00 P.M. On Sunday, hours are from 1:00 to 5:00 P.M. The site is closed on major holidays.

Fees: There is no admission charge for the lower grounds, gift shop, nature trail, and picnic areas, or for the self-guided tour (interpretive brochure provided).

Guided tour fees for the full tour are $5.00 for adults, $4.00 for seniors, $3.00 for children six to eighteen, and free for children five and under.

Tours of the Kershaw-Cornwallis House are $3.50 for adults and seniors, $1.00 for children six to eighteen, and free for children five and under.

How to get there: To reach Camden from the northeast, take Interstate 95 south to Florence. From Florence, take Interstate 20 west. Go about 45 miles to exit 98. From the ramp, bear right onto U.S. Highway 521 north toward Camden. Historic Camden's main entrance is 1.4 miles on the right, at 222 Broad Street.

From the south, take I–95 north to Interstate 26. Take I–26 to Columbia, then I–20 east to Camden. Take exit 98, and follow the directions given above.

From the west take I–26 or I–20 to Columbia, then take I–20 east to exit 98 for Camden, and follow the directions given above.

Stamping Locations and What the Cancellations Say

Ticket office/gift shop
222 Broad Street
(803) 432–9831

☐ Historic Camden Revolutionary War Site/Camden, SC ⏻

54 Kings Mountain National Military Park

Blacksburg, South Carolina
(864) 936–7921
www.nps.gov/kimo
Eastern time zone

Number of cancellations: One for the park, and one for Overmountain Victory National Historic Trail

Difficulty: Easy

About this site: The patriots turned the tide on the loyalists in the fight for independence on October 7, 1780, when a crushing battle on Kings Mountain essentially eliminated Lord Charles Cornwallis's left wing and forced him to retreat into South Carolina. The American victory slowed the British advance into North Carolina. The skirmish at Kings Mountain also set events in motion that would weaken British forces further with each ensuing battle, ending with Cornwallis's surrender to General Washington at Yorktown one year later.

❶ Don't miss this! Wayside exhibits explain the battle to you as you walk the self-guiding 1.5-mile loop trail through the battlefield. But to better understand how patriot militia trounced British Major Patrick Ferguson so effectively on these lands, be sure to see the twenty-seven-minute movie and the exhibits in the visitor center before your walk.

Hours: The site is open daily year-round, from 9:00 A.M. to 5:00 P.M. It is closed Thanksgiving, Christmas, and New Year's Day.

Fees: Admission to the park is free.

How to get there: From Greenville, take Interstate 85 north to North Carolina exit 2. From Charlotte, North Carolina, travel south on I–85 to exit 2. Continue southeast on South Carolina 216 to the park at 2625 Park Road.

Stamping Locations and What the Cancellations Say
Kings Mountain Visitor Center

☐ Kings Mountain Nat'l Military Park/Blacksburg, SC **❶**

☐ Overmountain Victory Nat'l Hist. Trail/South Carolina **❶**

55 Ninety Six National Historic Site

Ninety Six, South Carolina
(864) 543–4068
www.nps.gov/nisi
Eastern time zone

Number of cancellations: One

Difficulty: Easy

About this site: Among the more popular theories about how this battlefield got its name is this: In the early 1700s, English traders who walked these lands named this small settlement for the number of miles northwest they would have to travel to reach the Cherokee village of Keowee. It turned out that they were wrong about the distance, but the name stuck. European and African-American settlers established a pioneer town, building a fort and battling Cherokees in the French and Indian War. Later, loyalists attacked in the first Revolutionary War battle south of New England, kindling pre-Declaration of Independence hostilities in 1775.

The British returned in 1780 and fortified Ninety Six as a strategically advantageous stronghold. Suddenly, Ninety Six found itself in the midst of a four-week-long siege as General

Nathanael Greene led 1,000 patriot troops against 550 redcoats, who defended the town from May 22 to June 18, 1781. It was the longest siege of the Revolution (outside of a city), but the out-manned loyalists finally exhausted the patriots and won the battle, one of their last victories before the October 1781 surrender.

❶ Don't miss this! If you've never seen a military mine—and chances are good that you haven't—there's one at Ninety Six, engineered by Colonel Thaddeus Kosciuszko as a way to tunnel under the British-controlled fort during the 1781 siege and blast through the earthen walls of the redcoat outpost. Before the patriots could carry out their plan, however, loyalists discovered them, and nearly every patriot "sapper" (trench digger) was killed in the skirmish—with the exception of Kosciuszko himself, who was wounded but survived. Kosciuszko's engineering skills are widely credited for American military successes throughout the Revolution, especially at Saratoga. Most of the 90-foot tunnel survives, the only one remaining from the Revolutionary War.

Hours: The site is open daily year-round, from 8:00 A.M. to 5:00 P.M. It is closed Thanksgiving, Christmas, and New Year's Day. While the gates close promptly at 5:00 P.M., visitors who park outside the gate are welcome to stay until sunset.

Fees: Admission to the park is free.

How to get there: From Interstate 26 at the Newberry exit, take South Carolina 34 to the town of Ninety Six. Turn left at the second traffic light by the town's fountain, and follow signs to the park.

From Interstate 20, take U.S. Highway 25 north to the junction with U.S. Business Highway 221. Take US 221 north and east to the intersection with South Carolina 34; turn right on SC 34, and continue to the town of Ninety Six. In town, turn right on South Carolina 246. Drive south on SC 246 to the park.

Stamping Locations and What the Cancellations Say
Visitor center

☐ Ninety Six Nat'l Historic Site/Ninety Six, SC **❶**

Columbia, South Carolina
(864) 338–4841
www.sc-heritagecorridor.org
Eastern time zone

Number of cancellations: Two

Difficulty: Tricky

About this site: Stretching through fourteen counties on the southwestern side of South Carolina, this heritage corridor captures the historic and present-day cultures and attractions of the mountainous up country, and the low country's agricultural communities, industrial villages, and cities. This cross-section of South Carolina history begins in Charleston, commemorating its role in the Revolutionary and Civil Wars, and spreads northwestward with more than fifty stops along two recommended touring routes, one for historical and cultural discovery and the other for natural settings and surroundings. Visitors find insights about the area's farming communities, its African-American history from slavery to freedom, and South Carolina's migration from being a producer of rice, indigo, and cotton to today's manufacturing and major agricultural activity.

Don't miss this! Region 2—from Abbeville and Greenwood to Johnson—provides several unusual and fun places to stop. The Gardens of Park Seed Company provide a living demonstration of the products developed by one of the world's largest flower and vegetable seed packagers. Visit from May to July to see the spectacular flower gardens at their brilliant peak.

Just down the road, make a stop at Emerald Farm, where you can see the much-acclaimed Sannen Goat Milk Soap being made and purchase some of this gentle concoction, said to be especially good for rejuvenation of dry skin. You can pet goats and sheep here, and even try milking a goat.

In Region 3, the most famous draw is the Thoroughbred Hall of Fame in Aiken, where some of the world's fastest and most venerated horses receive the recognition they deserve. You may recognize some of the names: Kelso, a five-time national champion, and Pleasant Colony, winner of the 1981 Kentucky Derby and Preakness Stakes. All kinds of racing memorabilia are collected here, from silks to trophies, and an unusually large assortment of paintings, sculptures, and photographs celebrate Aiken's history as a center of thoroughbred breeding and training. Call (803) 642–7630 for seasons, hours, and more information.

Hours: The Region 2 and Region 3 Discovery Centers are open year-round, Tuesday through Saturday, from 10:00 A.M. to 5:00 P.M. They are closed Sunday, Monday, and on major holidays.

Fees: Admission to the discovery centers is free. Many other sites in the South Carolina National Heritage Corridor charge admission fees; check the corridor's Web site for details.

How to get there: Directions to each cancellation stamping location are provided in the Stamping Locations section.

Stamping Locations and What the Cancellations Say

Joanne T. Rainsford Region 2 Discovery Center
405 Main Street, Edgefield, South Carolina
(803) 637–0877
From Interstate 20, take U.S. Highway 25 north about 15 miles into Edgefield. US 25 becomes Main Street, and the center is located between Johnson Street and Bacon Street on Main.

☐ South Carolina National Heritage Corridor/Edgefield, SC **❶**

Region 3 Discovery Center
87 Heritage Road, Blackville, South Carolina
(803) 284–3976
From Interstate 95, take U.S. Highway 78 (exit 77) toward Branchville/Bamberg. Follow US 78 west through Blackville to Reynold. Turn left on Melody Lane (South Carolina 6/528), and take the first right onto Heritage Road.

☐ SCNHC Region 3 Discovery Center/Blackville, SC **❶**

Tennessee

57 Andrew Johnson National Historic Site

Greeneville, Tennessee
(423) 638–3551
www.nps.gov/anjo
Eastern time zone

Number of cancellations: Two

Difficulty: Easy

About this site: When Abraham Lincoln's assassination abruptly made Andrew Johnson the seventeenth president of the United States, he faced a newly reunited nation in turmoil, the reconstruction of the war-devastated South, and racial discrimination against millions of freed black slaves. The former governor of Tennessee moved swiftly to carry out Lincoln's plans for full restoration of the South's rights as American states, but the South responded by restricting the former slaves' rights and denying them the vote. Johnson quickly became embroiled in controversy with Congress over his lenient Reconstruction policies. All of this presented enough challenge for any president . . . but Johnson faced more animosity when his firing of Secretary of War Edwin Stanton provoked the House of Representatives to impeach him on February 24, 1868.

This recently renovated home in Greeneville served as the Johnson family homestead, where he worked as a tailor before his political life began.

Don't miss this! Did Johnson commit "high crimes and misdemeanors" when he fired Stanton? Make your own decision about the president's guilt or innocence when you tour the visitor center. At the entrance, you'll receive a replica of an 1868 impeachment ticket, with which you can cast your own vote once you've explored the center and learned more about the circumstances leading up to Johnson's impeachment. Stop and make your choice at the One Vote Counts exhibit before you leave the center.

Hours: The site is open daily year-round, from 9:00 A.M. to 5:00 P.M. It is closed Thanksgiving, Christmas, and New Year's Day.

Fees: Admission to this park is free.

How to get there: The visitor center is located on the corner of College and Depot Streets in Greeneville.

From Interstate 81 southbound, take exit 36 to Tennessee 172. Follow TN 172 south to Greeneville.

From I–81 northbound, take exit 23 to U.S. Highway 11E. Follow US 11E north to Greeneville.

Once in Greenville, turn south/east onto US Business 11E (West Summer Street), and continue to U.S. Highway 321 (Main Street). Turn left. Turn right onto Depot Street at the next traffic light. Cross College Street at the stop sign, and turn left into the site's parking lot.

Stamping Locations and What the Cancellations Say
Johnson Visitor Center

☐ Andrew Johnson NHS/Greeneville, TN **⓪**

☐ Andrew Johnson NHS/Tailor Shop **⓪**

🄸 Big South Fork National River and Recreation Area

Oneida, Tennessee
(423) 286–7275
www.nps.gov/biso
Eastern time zone

Number of cancellations: One, plus additional cancellations in Kentucky

Difficulty: Easy

About this site: The Clear Fork River and the New River slice through the Cumberland Plateau and join to form the Big South Fork of the Cumberland River, the centerpiece of this recreation area. Not so long ago, logging operations conducted selective and clear cutting in this area, and deep coal mining was a major industry here. Today flourishing hillsides have replaced the logging operations and mining towns, and thriving vegetation helps keep the river and its tributaries clear and sparkling.

Hiking or horseback-riding adventures on Big South Fork's trails lead you to dramatic cliffs, astounding rock formations, and precarious-looking arches, while evidence of prehistoric life in this rugged countryside still exists within the park's rock shelters and campsites.

Don't miss this! While natural arches are almost commonplace in the American West, they're rare in the eastern states, and Big South Fork preserves more stone arches than you'll find anywhere else in the East. Follow the Twin Arches Trail less than a mile to see the largest of these formations, created by thousands of years of erosion. The Twin Arches Trail also winds past excellent examples of the park's many rock shelters, some of which served as naturally formed seasonal campsites for ancient tribal cultures.

The Big South Fork recreation area also reaches into Kentucky; additional stamping sites are listed in the Kentucky chapter of this guide.

Hours: The park is open daily year-round, from 8:00 A.M. to 4:00 P.M. It is closed Christmas.

Fees: Admission to this park is free.

How to get there: From Interstate 75 southbound, take Kentucky 461 south to Kentucky 80. Take KY 80 west to U.S. Highway 27. Follow US 27 south to Oneida, and follow Tennessee 297 west into the park.

From I–75 northbound, take Tennessee 63 west to US 27. Follow US 27 north to Oneida, and follow TN 297 west into the park.

From Interstate 40 westbound, exit at US 27, travel north to Oneida, and follow TN 297 west into the park.

From I–40 eastbound, exit at U.S. Highway 127, and travel north to Tennessee 154. Follow TN 154 north to TN 297, and take TN 297 east into the park.

Stamping Locations and What the Cancellations Say

Bandy Creek Visitor Center

(423) 286–7275

From the park's entrance on TN 297, drive into the park to the Bandy Creek campground road. Turn left and continue to the visitor center.

☐ Big South Fork Nat'l River & Rec. Area/Oneida, TN Ⓤ

---

59 Chickamauga and Chattanooga National Military Park

Lookout Mountain, Tennessee
(423) 821–7786
www.nps.gov/chch
Eastern time zone

Number of cancellations: One for the park, plus a cancellation for the Trail of Tears National Historic Trail. More cancellations are available in the park's Georgia unit.

Difficulty: Easy

About this site: The 1863 Campaign for Chattanooga, one of the hardest fought campaigns of the Civil War, came to a close here in November 1863, as more than 150,000 Union and Confederate soldiers fought for control of the important railroad hub in Chattanooga. Three bloody days of fighting resulted in some 34,000 casualties, and it seemed as though the Confederate Army of Tennessee would win the battle, but Union General Ulysses S. Grant arrived with reinforcements and drove the Confederates down from Lookout Mountain and Missionary Ridge. Chattanooga became a Union stronghold from which the army would engineer its drive across Georgia the following year.

 Don't miss this! Taking the incline train to the top of Lookout Mountain from its terminus on Tennessee 17 (Tennessee Avenue) is a relaxing and uncommonly scenic way to visit this unit of the military park. The train arrives just 0.2 of a mile from Point Park and the Lookout Mountain Battlefield Visitor Center, and you'll have the opportunity to linger over the spectacular view of the city of Chattanooga, the Moccasin Bend of the Tennessee River, and adjoining Chattanooga Creek.

Hours: The battlefield grounds are open during daylight hours except for Point Park, which is open from 9:00 A.M. to one hour before sunset daily. The visitor center is open daily from 8:30 A.M. to 5:00 P.M. It is closed Christmas.

Fees: No admission is charged at the Lookout Mountain Visitor Center. Point Park charges a $3.00 per day usage fee per person; children sixteen and under are free.

How to get there: From Nashville, take Interstate 24 south to exit 174, and then continue south on U.S. Highway 41. Take Tennessee 148 to the top of Lookout Mountain, and turn right on East Brow Road. Point Park and the Lookout Mountain Visitor Center are at the end of East Brow Road.

Stamping Locations and What the Cancellations Say

Lookout Mountain Battlefield Visitor Center
(423) 821–7786
Located across from the Point Park entrance

☐ ChCh NMP Lookout Mtn. Battlefield/Lookout Mtn, TN ⓤ

☐ Trail of Tears National Historic Trail/Georgia ⓓ

60 Fort Donelson National Battlefield

Dover, Tennessee
(931) 232–5706 ext. 0
www.nps.gov/fodo
Central time zone

Number of cancellations: One, plus one for the Underground Railroad

Difficulty: Easy

About this site: General Ulysses S. Grant burst through the southern defenses at Forts Henry and Heiman and moved swiftly to overpower Fort Donelson during the February 1862 Henry–Donelson Campaign. The Union general delivered a destructive blow that forced Confederate General Simon B. Buckner to acquiesce to Grant's now-famous pronouncement: "No terms except an unconditional and immediate surrender can be accepted." The Confederate defenses fell, and Grant reclaimed the heart of the Confederacy for the Union.

❶ Don't miss this! Take the 6-mile self-guided auto tour after you've viewed the fifteen-minute video at the visitor center. The battle's significance in the overall conflict becomes clear when you've viewed this presentation.

Hours: The battlefield is open daily from 8:00 A.M. to 4:30 P.M. It is closed Christmas.

Fees: Admission to the park is free.

How to get there: From Nashville, take Interstate 24 west to Clarksville (exit 4). Turn left on Wilma Rudolph Boulevard and continue for about 3 miles. Stay on this highway until you reach 101st Airborne Division Parkway. Turn right at this intersection; this parkway will change into Tennessee 374. From TN 374, turn right on U.S. Highway 79 southbound. Follow the signs to Dover (approximately 30 miles). The visitor center is 1 mile west of the town.

Stamping Locations and What the Cancellations Say
Fort Donelson Visitor Center

☐ Fort Donelson National Battlefield/Dover, TN ❶
☐ Fort Donelson NB/Underground RR Freedom Network ❶

61 Great Smoky Mountains National Park

Gatlinburg, Tennessee
(865) 436–1200
www.nps.gov/grsm
Eastern time zone

Number of cancellations: Eight for the park, plus a cancellation for the Trail of Tears National Historic Trail. An additional cancellation is available in North Carolina.

Difficulty: Challenging

About this site: More people visit Great Smoky Mountains National Park each year than any other national park in the nation—and once you've seen this park, the numbers are no longer a surprise. For year-round attraction, endless variety, and sheer visual satisfaction, the Great Smokies are unsurpassed in

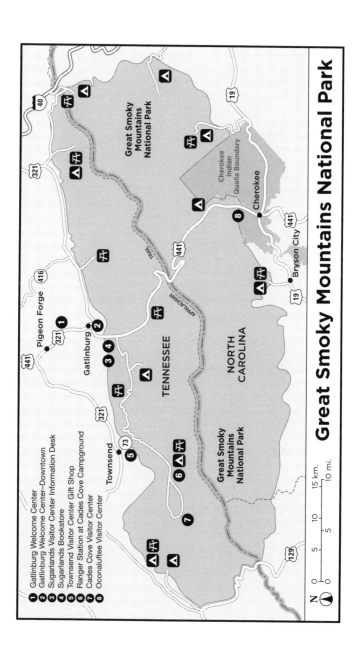

Great Smoky Mountains National Park

1 Gatlinburg Welcome Center
2 Gatlinburg Welcome Center–Downtown
3 Sugarlands Visitor Center Information Desk
4 Sugarlands Bookstore
5 Townsend Visitor Center Gift Shop
6 Ranger Station at Cades Cove Campground
7 Cades Cove Visitor Center
8 Oconaluftee Visitor Center

their ability to take a day, a weekend, or a week of exploration and pack it full of activity, historical discovery, and natural wonder.

Stamping tips: It's not hard to get any of these individual cancellations, as all the visitor centers are open year-round and even the ranger station at Cades Cove Campground keeps regular hours. But this is a big park with a great deal to see and do, and you'll want to make the most of your time here by exploring the wilderness and the historic sites. Plan your stamping around your recreational activities instead of the other way around. The combination of fabulous scenic vistas, unmatched diversity of wildlife, and inevitable traffic and delays will only frustrate you if you attempt to rush from one visitor center to the next.

Visitor centers all close earlier in winter. If you're not sure you'll make it to the center of your choice before it closes, call ahead to check the closing time, as these will vary with the location and inclement weather patterns.

Additional cancellations are available in the North Carolina portion of the park; see the North Carolina chapter of this guide for more information.

Don't miss this! Nine million people visit this park each year! Despite its wilderness setting and its park-wide emphasis on natural resource recovery, the fact is that summer and fall weekends in the Great Smokies can bring bumper-to-bumper congestion and long waits to drive scenic roads. This being said, the park itself is more than half a million acres in size, so if you find your way into the backcountry, you can enjoy a wilderness experience even in the peak seasons. Day hiking and horseback riding, camping, fishing, and backpacking all help put some distance between yourself and the throngs, while providing long interludes during which you can gaze into the blue-gray vastness that gives the Smokies their name.

Clingmans Dome, the highest peak in the Great Smoky Mountains at 6,643 feet, is also the most elevated point on the Appalachian Trail. Clingmans presents hikers with a particularly challenging climb that ends with a tremendous reward: The view of the mountain range and surrounding countryside from here is one of the best in the park.

Hours: Sevierville Visitor Center is open daily year-round, Monday to Saturday from 8:30 A.M. to 5:30 P.M., and Sunday from 9:00 A.M. to 6:00 P.M.

Gatlinburg Welcome Center is open daily year-round. From November to March, hours are from 8:00 A.M. to 5:30 P.M. From April through October, hours are from 8:00 A.M. to 7:00 P.M. Sunday through Thursday, and 8:00 A.M. to 9:00 P.M. Friday and Saturday.

Gatlinburg Welcome Center–Downtown is open daily year-round, from 10:00 A.M. to 6:00 P.M.

Sugarlands Visitor Center and bookstore are open daily year-round. Hours in April and May are from 8:00 A.M. to 6:00 P.M. From June to August, the center is open from 8:00 A.M. to 7:00 P.M. In September, hours are from 8:00 A.M. to 6:00 P.M. From December through February, hours are from 8:00 A.M. to 4:30 P.M. Hours in March are from 8:00 A.M. to 5:00 P.M.

Townsend Visitor Center is open daily year-round. In December and January, hours are from 9:00 a.m. to 4:30 P.M. In March, hours are 10:00 A.M. to 4:00 P.M. In April, May, and November, hours are 9:00 A.M. to 5:00 P.M. From June to October, hours are 9:00 A.M. to 6:00 P.M. The visitor center opens at noon on Sunday.

The **ranger station at Cades Cove** is open all year and staffed during daylight hours.

Cades Cove Visitor Center is open daily year-round. From April through August it is open from 9:00 A.M. to 7:00 P.M. In September and October, hours are from 9:00 A.M. to 6:00 P.M. In November, the center is open from 9:00 A.M. to 5:30 P.M. December and January hours are 9:00 A.M. to 4:30 P.M. In February, the center closes at 5:00 P.M., and in March, it remains open until 5:30 P.M. The center is closed Christmas.

Fees: Admission to the park is free.

How to get there: To reach the Gatlinburg entrance from Interstate 40, take exit 407 (Sevierville) to Tennessee 66 southbound, and continue to U.S. Highway 441. Follow US 441 south to the park.

To reach the Townsend entrance from I–40 in Knoxville, take exit 386B for U.S. Highway 129, which heads south to Alcoa/Maryville. At Maryville, proceed on U.S. Highway 321 north through Townsend. Continue straight on Tennessee 73 into the park.

Stamping Locations and What the Cancellations Say

The cancellations are listed in the order you will reach them if you take exit 407 on I–40 enter the park from Gatlinburg on US 441. Use the map to determine your route if you prefer to enter from

Townsend. If you're entering the park from US 129 at the Cherokee National Forest, simply reverse the order.

Sevierville Visitor Center

3099 Winfield Dunn Parkway, Sevierville
(865) 932–4650

☐ Great Smoky Mountains National Park/Sevierville Visitor
Center **①**

Gatlinburg Welcome Center

(865) 430–3112
Located on US 441 2 miles outside of Gatlinburg

☐ Great Smoky Mountains Nat'l Park/Gatlinburg, TN 37738 **①**

Gatlinburg Welcome Center–Downtown

(865) 436–0604
Located at traffic light 3 on the parkway in downtown Gatlinburg

☐ Great Smoky Mountains National Park/Gatlinburg,
TN 37738 **①**

Sugarlands Visitor Center information desk

(865) 436–1291
Located inside the park, 2 miles south of Gatlinburg on US 441

☐ Great Smoky Mountains National Park/Sugarland
VC/Tennessee **①**

☐ Trail of Tears National Historic Trail/Tennessee **①**

Sugarlands bookstore

(865) 436–1315
Located inside the Sugarlands Visitor Center

☐ Great Smoky Mountains National Park/Sugarlands
Visitor Center **①**

Townsend Visitor Center Gift Shop

7906 East Lamar Alexander Parkway
(865) 448–6134
Located on US 321 in Townsend. From Sugarlands, turn right at
the junction with TN 73, and left at the junction with US 321.

☐ Great Smoky Mountains National Park/Townsend,
TN 37882 **①**

Ranger station at Cades Cove Campground
(865) 448–2472

☐ Great Smoky Mountains National Park/CADES COVE/
   Tennessee Ⓓ

Cades Cove Visitor Center
Located inside the park near the midpoint of the 11-mile,
one-way Cades Cove Loop Road

☐ Great Smoky Mountains National Park/CADES COVE/
   Tennessee Ⓓ

62 Obed Wild and Scenic River

Wartburg, Tennessee
(423) 346–6294
www.nps.gov/obed
Eastern time zone

Number of cancellations: Two

Difficulty: Easy

About this site: The Obed River, Daddy's Creek, Clear Creek,
and the Emory River gradually converge along the 45-mile length
of this preserved area. Cascading down from the Cumberland
Plateau, the Obed drops precipitously over its protected length,
creating exciting whitewater with Class V rapids in the spring and
fall. Above the river, rocky gorge walls and impressive bluffs,
chiseled by the river's flow over the course of tens of thousands
of years, jut sharply upward in some of the most rugged rock formations in the nation's southeastern region.

Stamping tips: The park visitor center does us the courtesy of
keeping a duplicate cancellation outside the building for people
who arrive after hours. You'll find it in the "Brochures" holder by
the front door—just open the box. If you arrive during the visitor
center's open hours, get the cancellation at the front desk
because it's newer and will give you a clearer imprint.

❗ **Don't miss this!** If you're not up for whitewater rafting (bring your
own raft), consider hiking a segment of the Cumberland Trail that
follows part of the river. Beginning at the Nemo trailhead at the

Rock Creek Camp area (pick up a map at the visitor center), you'll enjoy a moderate hike with great views of the gorge, shorter glimpses of the river, and some not-so-distant archeology as you pass the remains of a strip mine. You can find more information about this trail at the Cumberland Trail Conference Web site at www.cumberlandtrail.org/obed.html.

Hours: The park is open daily year-round, from 8:00 A.M. to 4:30 P.M. It is closed Thanksgiving, Christmas Eve, Christmas Day, New Year's Eve, and New Year's Day.

Fees: Admission to the park is free.

How to get there: From Interstate 40 west of Knoxville, take U.S. Highway 27 north to the town of Wartburg. Turn west onto Kingston Street, and continue to the visitor center on North Maiden Street.

Stamping Locations and What the Cancellations Say

Inside visitor center
208 North Maiden Street, Wartburg

☐ Obed Wild and Scenic River/Wartburg, TN **Ⓓ**

Outside visitor center

☐ Obed Wild and Scenic River/Wartburg, TN **Ⓓ**

63 Shiloh National Military Park

Shiloh, Tennessee
731-689-5696, www.nps.gov/shil
Central time zone

Number of cancellations: One for the park, plus one for the Trail of Tears National Historic Trail. An additional cancellation is available in Mississippi.

Difficulty: Easy

About this site: On April 6 and 7, 1862, the Civil War expanded westward with the conflict at Shiloh. The battle for control of the Confederate railway system ended badly for the Southern troops, but both sides felt the losses, with nearly 24,000 soldiers dead, wounded, or missing before the bloody fighting came to an end.

❶ Don't miss this! The 10-mile auto tour has wayside exhibits that explain troop maneuvers during the two-day battle—but for a more in-depth understanding of the massive confrontation and its importance in the total context of the Civil War, purchase the CD audio tour and use it as a guide as you drive the loop. Nearly twenty-four thousand soldiers died or were wounded on these grounds, so it's worth taking the time to understand what was gained and lost on those days in 1862.

Hours: Shiloh National Military Park is open daily from 8:00 A.M. to 5:00 P.M. It is closed Christmas.

Fees: Admission is $5.00 per vehicle, good for seven days. Individuals on foot, bicycle, or motorcycle are admitted for $3.00 each, good for seven days.

How to get there: From Interstate 40 west of Nashville, exit at Lexington, and take Tennessee 22 south to Shiloh Battlefield. From Memphis, take Tennessee 57 east to TN 22, and head north to Shiloh Battlefield. The visitor center is 1 mile east of the main entrance on TN 22.

Stamping Locations and What the Cancellations Say

Shiloh National Military Park Visitor Center bookstore
1055 Pittsburg Landing Road, Shiloh
(731) 689–3475

☐ Shiloh NMP/Shiloh, TN ❶

☐ Trail of Tears National Historic Trail/NC, GA, TN, KY, IL, MO, OK, AR ❶

64 Stones River National Battlefield

Murfreesboro, Tennessee
(615) 893–9501 weekdays,
(615) 478–1035 on weekends and holidays
www.nps.gov/stri
Central time zone

Number of cancellations: One for the battlefield, plus cancellations for the Trail of Tears National Historic Trail, the Underground Railroad, and the Tennessee Civil War National Heritage Area

Difficulty: Easy

About this site: After the Confederate army defeated the Union at Fredericksburg, morale plummeted throughout the North—and with the approach of the Emancipation Proclamation's effective date of January 1, 1863, President Abraham Lincoln needed a triumph, and fast. He charged General William Rosencrans's army in Tennessee with providing a win that would boost Union spirits and turn the war back in their favor.

Rosencrans responded by splitting his army into three branches and marching to find General Braxton Bragg's rebel troops. The attack came on the frosty morning of December 31, 1862, and continued for three days... and before it ended, 23,500 men were dead or wounded, including 1,800 Confederate soldiers who encountered fifty-seven Union cannons on the west bank of the Stones River. General Bragg retreated as the Union marched triumphantly into Murfreesboro.

Don't miss this! Stones River National Cemetery holds the graves of 6,100 Union soldiers who died at Stones River and in Murfreesboro, Franklin, Shelbyville, Tullahoma, and Cowan, all of whom were moved here in 1865 and 1866. If you have a Union ancestor who fought in the southern campaign, you can search for a specific soldier by name at www.stonesrivernc.org, and then find his gravesite on the cemetery map before you visit the park. The site provides the soldier's regiment and company, rank, date and place of death, and his home state to help you match your genealogical information with the database.

Hours: The site is open daily from 8:00 A.M. to 5:00 P.M. It is closed Christmas.

Fees: Admission to the park is free.

How to get there: From Interstate 24 south of Nashville, take exit 76B. Follow Medical Center Parkway to its intersection with Thompson Lane. Turn left and continue to the Old Nashville Highway ramp. Turn right onto the ramp, turn left onto Old Nashville Highway, and follow the signs to the battlefield at 3501 Old Nashville Highway.

Stamping Locations and What the Cancellations Say

Visitor center

☐ Stones River National Battlefield/Murfreesboro, TN ❶

☐ Trail of Tears National Historic Trail/Tennessee Ⓓ

☐ Stones River NB/Underground RR Freedom Network Ⓤ

☐ Tennessee Civil War NHA/Murfreesboro, TN Ⓓ

65 Tennessee Civil War National Heritage Area

Tennessee NPS Affiliated Area
Murfreesboro, Tennessee
(615) 898–2947
histpres.mtsu.edu/tncivwar
Central time zone

Number of cancellations: Three

Difficulty: Tricky

About this site: Beyond the troop movements, the battles, the monuments, and the famous commanders' names, a deeper story unfolded in the state of Tennessee during the Civil War's approach, its reality, and the lingering aftermath of Reconstruction. The Tennessee Civil War National Heritage Area links organizations, historic sites, and people from all over the state in telling the complex tale of personal struggle and transformation during a time dubbed "America's Greatest Challenge," the quarter-century from 1850 to 1875. National park battlefields provide Tennessee's wartime perspective, while the national heritage area preserves the state's civilian point of view during occupation by Union forces, the height of the Underground Railroad, the dramatic decline in farming's viability without slaves, and the stunning transformations that occurred during political and social Reconstruction.

Stamping tips: When you visit this office, ask for heritage area manager Laura Holder, who is the person most familiar with the Passport program.

Note the limited hours (no weekends, closed on campus holidays) of the Center for Historic Preservation, and schedule your visit accordingly.

❶ **Don't miss this!** While the area itself is in its formative stages, the heritage area manager suggests that you connect your Passport cancellation stop with one of several sites in the Murfreesboro area, a city that shifted from Confederate to Union control and back repeatedly during the war.

The Rutherford County Courthouse in the Murfreesboro Public Square still serves as the county office building, but during the Civil War, it functioned alternately as a watchtower, a prison, a Union headquarters, a hospital, and even a ballroom. Surrounding the courthouse is the East Main Street Historic District, much of which dates back to the Civil War era and earlier in this city's history. Walking tour maps of this eleven-block area are available in many inns and public buildings, with listings of antebellum and Reconstruction-era homes and commercial buildings to view as you wander through the charming neighborhood.

Hours and fees: The Center for Historic Preservation office on the Middle Tennessee State University campus is open year-round, Monday to Friday, from 8:00 A.M. to 4:30 P.M. It is closed for campus holidays; call to check before visiting during college breaks and holiday weeks. Admission to this office is free. The Heritage Center of Murfreesboro and Rutherford County is open Monday to Friday, from 9:00 A.M. to 3:00 P.M. Tours are available on Sunday with advance reservations. Admission is free.

Stones River National Battlefield is open daily from 8:00 A.M. to 5:00 P.M. It is closed Christmas. Admission is free.

How to get there: To reach the stamping site at Middle Tennessee University from Interstate 24 south of Nashville, take exit 81 to Shelby Street. Follow Shelby Street to South Church Street, and turn right on South Church. Continue on South Church to Main Street, and turn right on Main Street. Building 60 is at 1421 East Main Street.

Stamping Locations and What the Cancellations Say

Center for Historic Preservation
Middle Tennessee State University, 1417 East Main Street, Murfreesboro

☐ Tennessee Civil War NHA/Murfreesboro, TN Ⓓ

Heritage Center of Murfreesboro and Rutherford County
225 West College Street, Murfreesboro
(615) 217–8013

☐ Tennessee Civil War NHA/Murfreesboro, TN Ⓓ

Stones River National Battlefield
Visitor center
3501 Old Nashville Highway, Murfreesboro
(615) 393–9501 weekdays; (615) 478–1035 weekends
and holidays

☐ Tennessee Civil War NHA/Murfreesboro, TN **Ⓓ**

☐ Stones River National Battlefield/Murfreesboro, TN **Ⓤ**

☐ Stones River NB/Underground RR Freedom Network **Ⓤ**

☐ Trail of Tears National Historic Trail/Tennessee **Ⓓ**

Virgin Islands

Easy or heroic? While you need to leave the continental United States by boat or airline to visit the Virgin Islands, none of these options carries with it the potential for discomfort, fear, or any hardship that might earn "Heroic" status for other Passport stamping trips. The difficulty ratings attached to Virgin Island stamping sites are based on the ease of cancellation stamp collection once you've arrived on the islands.

66 Buck Island Reef National Monument

Christiansted, Saint Croix, Virgin Islands
(340) 773–1460
www.nps.gov/buis
Atlantic time zone

Number of cancellations: Two for the monument, plus four cancellations for other national parks

Difficulty: Easy

About this site: The whole island is only 176 acres, but it's not the island that draws visitors to this undeveloped corner of the Caribbean every day—it's the elkhorn coral barrier reef that surrounds it, a thriving ecosystem chock-a-block with undersea wildlife. Home to endangered species including hawksbill turtles, the island's quiet waters and barrier reef provide both underwater paradise and critical habitat for plants, birds, fish, crustaceans, and multicelled creatures, most of which can be seen by snorkeling or scuba diving the park's underwater trail.

Stamping tips: While there are restrooms on Buck Island, there is no visitor center or ranger station, so the cancellations for this park are at Christiansted National Historic Site. Given that the island excursions offered by concessionaires are either full-day or half-day tours, plan to get these cancellations on another day, or in the morning before a half-day afternoon trip.

Don't miss this! If you've never snorkeled before, Buck Island is the place to start, because you mustn't leave the island before you've seen the park's famous underwater trail through its expansive coral reef. Led by one of the many concessionaires' tour guides, you'll float on top of barely aqua-tinted water (12 to 18 feet deep) and see dozens of varieties of brightly colored fish, stands of coral in deep, rich shades of yellow and orange, and underwater creatures like sponges, stingrays, jellyfish, and sea urchins, all in a world that's invisible from the beach or the boat deck. Even landlubbers like me can be comfortable with the use of flotation devices—now required for every snorkeler—so there's no reason to miss out on this extraordinary experience if you're not a swimmer.

Hours: The park is open daily year-round, from 8:00 A.M. to 5:00 P.M. It is closed Thanksgiving, Christmas, and New Year's Day.

Fees: Admission to the park is free. Fees are charged for passage to the island by boat.

How to get there: From the airport or marina, travel by car or taxi van to downtown Christiansted or to Green Cay Marina east of Christiansted. There are six concession companies that provide transport by boat to Buck Island Reef National Monument from these locations. Each offers full-day or half-day trips, many of which include snorkeling instruction and guided snorkeling tours. More information on these concessions is available at www.gotostcroix.com.

Stamping Locations and What the Cancellations Say

Scale House Visitor Center
Christiansted National Historic Site
(340) 773–1460

☐ Buck Island Reef National Monument/C'sted St. Croix, USVI ❶

☐ Christiansted National Historic Site/C'sted St. Croix, USVI ❶

☐ Salt River Bay, NHP/Christiansted, St. Croix, V.I. ❶

Fort Christiansvaern

Christiansted National Historic Site

☐ Buck Island Reef National Monument/C'sted St. Croix,
USVI 00820 **⓪**

☐ Christiansted National Historic Site/C'sted St. Croix,
USVI 00820 **⓪**

☐ Salt River Bay, NHP/Christiansted, St. Croix, V.I. **◑**

67 Christiansted National Historic Site

Christiansted, Saint Croix, Virgin Islands
(340) 773–1460
www.nps.gov/chri
Atlantic time zone

Number of cancellations: Two for the site, plus two for Buck
Island Reef National Monument and two for Salt River Bay
National Historical Park

Difficulty: Easy

About this site: For nearly two centuries, from 1733 until 1917,
the town of Christiansted served as the capital of the Danish
West Indies—islands that first included Saint Thomas and Saint
John in the 1600s, and then expanded with the addition of Saint
Croix in 1733, when the Danish West India and Guinea Company
purchased the island from the French. Sold to the king of Den-
mark in 1754, the islands enjoyed a peaceful existence except for
short interludes of British occupation in the early 1800s.

Christiansted fell on hard times when the Danish government
abolished slavery, but it would be decades before the United
States purchased the islands for $25 million in 1917.

❗ **Don't miss this!** Your Christiansted experience will take you onto
the St. Croix Heritage Trail, where you'll discover more Danish
history in the many carefully preserved churches, government
buildings, and museums intermingled with modern shops and
restaurants—many of which are in Danish-period buildings. Fans
of neoclassic architecture will enjoy the Government House, and
the earliest definition of island culture comes through in the
shaded walkways and the waterfront square.

Hours: The site is open daily year-round, Monday through Friday, from 8:00 A.M. to 5:00 P.M., and Saturday and Sunday from 9:00 A.M. to 5:00 P.M.

Fees: Admission is $3.00 per person to tour the fort.

How to get there: From the airport, take the Melvin Evans Highway (Route 66) east to Route 70 east into the historic town of Christiansted. The park is located at the bottom of King Street, before King's Wharf at Christiansted Harbor.

Stamping Locations and What the Cancellations Say
Scale House Visitor Center

☐ Christiansted National Historic Site/C'sted St. Croix, USVI ➊

☐ Buck Island Reef National Monument/C'sted St. Croix, USVI ➊

☐ Salt River Bay, NHP/Christiansted, St. Croix, V.I. ➋

Fort Christiansvaern

☐ Christiansted National Historic Site/C'sted St. Croix,
USVI 00820 ➊

☐ Buck Island Reef National Monument/C'sted St. Croix,
USVI 00820 ➊

☐ Salt River Bay, NHP/Christiansted, St. Croix, V.I. ➋

68 Salt River Bay National Historical Park and Ecological Preserve

Christiansted, Saint Croix, Virgin Islands
(340) 773–1460
www.nps.gov/sari
Atlantic time zone

Number of cancellations: Three for the park, plus four cancellations for other parks at Christiansted cancellation locations

Difficulty: Tricky

About this site: Christopher Columbus landed here on November 14, 1493, and the chilly reception he received from the native Caribs gave the Bay of Arrows at Salt River Bay its name. If you need more justification than this for spending time in this wild, remote place, the remarkable park bears evidence of thousands of years of human history: Ancient Indian civilizations, Spanish domination, a series of failed European colonies, and the slaves Europeans brought from Africa have left behind clues to their experience—all within just over a thousand acres of mangrove forests, coral reefs, and submarine canyons.

Stamping tips: If you're content to pick up your cancellation at Christiansted instead of at the Salt River Bay Visitor Center, you'll have no trouble getting the cancellation. The new visitor center at the preserve, opened in 2006, may be closed during the off-season (summer through early October) when visitation drops to a minimum. However, the cancellation at the center is a duplicate of the two available at Christiansted.

❶ Don't miss this! If you don't have a car, several concessionaires on Saint Croix offer guided land tours of Salt River Bay, as well as hiking tours, snorkeling and scuba diving, and kayaking tours. If you're looking to tour by water, visit Caribbean Adventure Tours at www.tourcarib.com, or call 340–778–1522. Be sure to ask about after-dark kayak tours to view the water's eerie glitter in the moonlight. Park rangers often lead hiking tours for groups, so call the park for more information on what's available during your scheduled visit.

Hours: Christiansted National Historic Site is open daily year-round, Monday through Friday, from 8:00 A.M. to 5:00 P.M., and Saturday and Sunday from 9:00 A.M. to 5:00 P.M.

Salt River Bay Visitor Center is open daily in fall, winter, and spring from 8:30 A.M. to 4:00 P.M. The center may be closed in the off-season (summer and early fall).

Fees: Admission to the park is free.

How to get there: The park is 5 miles from Christiansted National Historic Site and can be reached by car via Route 75 from Christiansted, connecting to Route 80.

Stamping Locations and What the Cancellations Say
Scale House Visitor Center
Christiansted National Historic Site

☐ Salt River Bay NHP/Christiansted, St. Croix, VI ❶

☐ Christiansted National Historic Site/C'sted St. Croix, USVI ❶

☐ Buck Island Reef National Monument/C'sted St. Croix, USVI ❶

Fort Christiansvaern

Christiansted National Historic Site

☐ Salt River Bay, NHP/Christiansted, St. Croix, V.I. **Ⓤ**

☐ Christiansted National Historic Site/C'sted St. Croix, USVI 00820 **Ⓤ**

☐ Buck Island Reef National Monument/C'sted St. Croix, USVI 00820 **Ⓤ**

Salt River Bay Visitor Center

☐ Salt River Bay NHP/Christiansted, St. Croix, V.I. **Ⓤ**

69 Virgin Islands National Park and Virgin Islands Coral Reef National Monument

Saint John, Virgin Islands
(340) 776–6201
www.nps.gov/viis and www.nps.gov/vicr
Atlantic time zone

Number of cancellations: Three

Difficulty: Tricky

About this site: You've found it! This is the tropical paradise you came to the Virgin Islands to enjoy. Coconut palm trees, island breezes, long stretches of dazzling white beaches, turquoise water twinkling in the sunlight . . . it's all here, and it's all part of a flourishing ecosystem that covers two-thirds of Saint John and supports more than 300 species of fish, fifty coral varieties, gorgonians, sponges, well over one hundred bird species, and nearly 750 different plants. Island mountains, the products of volcanic activity, seem to rise right out of the ocean with dramatic, 30-percent slopes from sea level to summit. Both dry and wet tropical forests exist side by side on this island, as do the remains of eighteenth- and nineteenth-century sugar plantations, and ancient petroglyphs that archeologists believe may be 3,000 years old.

More than 12,000 sensitive underwater acres form the Virgin Islands Coral Reef, giving back to the mangrove forests and sea grass beds that help sustain them by stemming the erosion produced by the region's frequent tropical storms and preventing the total obliteration of its neighboring bionetwork. Humpback and pilot whales, dolphins, pelicans, terns, and sea turtles all find the nourishment and habitat they need within the reef's protective boundary.

Stamping tips: It's easy enough to get the cancellation at the Cruz Bay Visitor Center. Volunteers staff the Eastern National Trunk Bay kiosk, so there's always a chance that you'll encounter a closed kiosk when you arrive—but given the popularity and year-round season at this park, chances are good that the kiosk will be open. As the cancellation there is a duplicate, you'll only be at risk if you're collecting an imprint from every existing cancellation stamp.

Don't miss this! If you want to lie on a beach and revel in the sun, sand, and surf, you've come to the right place. If you want to take a three-hour hike on the Reef Bay Trail and marvel at the inner workings of tropical forests, maybe catching a glimpse of a mongoose or a gecko, you can do that, too. Take a safari bus (that's a local taxi) to one of the more remote parts of the island and see archeological ruins, or rent a small sailboat and try one-handing it on the gentle waves. You won't be at a loss for diversions at this park.

The Virgin Islands Coral Reef overlaps Virgin Islands National Park at Coral Harbor and Ram's Head, giving you land access to the monument's general acreage. But if you really want to experience the reef, you'll have to don a mask and snorkel its waters, making visual contact with its bounty of undersea creatures.

Several beaches on Saint John's south shore provide snorkeling access to the reef: Salt Pond Bay, where you can swim out to a set of jagged rocks covered with corals and inhabited by interesting fish; or Little Lameshur Bay, where beginners will find a cluster of rocks and coral fairly close to shore. More experienced snorkelers can swim out from along the western shoreline to Europa Bay and gaze down into deep water that's bustling with schools of fish among the coral cliffs.

Hours: The park is open twenty-four hours a day, seven days a week, year-round.

Cruz Bay Visitor Center is open daily year-round, from 8:00 A.M. to 4:30 P.M. It is closed Christmas.

Eastern National Trunk Bay kiosk is open daily year-round, from 8:00 A.M. to 4:30 P.M. It is closed Christmas.

Fees: Admission to the park is free. A same-day usage fee is charged at Trunk Bay: $4.00 for adults, free for children sixteen and under.

How to get there: Access to the park is by boat only. Hourly ferry service from Red Hook, Saint Thomas (a twenty-minute ride) is available and operates starting at 6:30 A.M., then departs on the hour from 7:00 A.M. to midnight. Ferry service from Saint John to Saint Thomas runs on the hour from 6:00 A.M. to 11:00 P.M. Less frequent ferries travel between Charlotte Amalie, Saint Thomas, and Saint John (a forty-five-minute ride).

Stamping Locations and What the Cancellations Say

Cruz Bay Visitor Center
(340) 776–6201 ext. 238

☐ V.I. National Park/St. John, V.I. **❶**

☐ V.I. Coral Reef National Monument/St. John, V.I. **❷**

Eastern National kiosk
Trunk Bay
(340) 714–4836

☐ V.I. Coral Reef National Monument/St. John, V.I. **❷**

National Trails that Cross Multiple States

70 Natchez Trace Parkway and Natchez Trace National Scenic Trail

Tupelo, Mississippi
(800) 305–7417
www.nps.gov/natr and www.nps.gov/natt
Central time zone

Number of cancellations: Six for the parkway and trail, plus four cancellations for other parks

Difficulty: Easy to get unique cancellations, but challenging to collect all duplicates

About this site: Four-hundred and forty-four miles long and loaded with history and beautiful vistas, the Natchez Trace Parkway follows a route used first by buffalo, then by Native Americans of the Choctaw and Chickasaw Nations as they traversed Mississippi northward to reach salt licks in Tennessee. In the late 1700s, traders from the Ohio Valley traveled down the Mississippi River by boat, then sold their boats rather than fight the river's strong downstream currents on the return trip, traveling northward on the trace on foot. When steamboats made the upstream trip navigable, and as other roads were constructed, the trace faded away into antiquity until it emerged as a national park unit in 1938.

The Natchez Trace National Scenic Trail currently offers 65 miles of usable trail in four sections along the parkway, giving hikers a safe, off-road route from which they can take full advantage of the natural areas and historic sites along the trace.

Stamping tips: Keep in mind that the speed limit is 50 miles per hour on the Natchez Trace Parkway. This scenic road encourages a leisurely pace instead of a frantic rush from cancellation to cancellation, so you should plan at least two days, and maybe three, to drive the parkway from end to end.

The Natchez Trace Parkway Visitor Center in Tupelo is a productive cancellation stamp collecting spot, so you can gain cancellations that are not available anywhere else. Several other national park units are found within a short distance of Natchez Trace, so you can make the most of your parkway drive with side trips to Brices Cross Roads National Battlefield Site, Tupelo National Battlefield, Natchez National Historical Park, and Vicksburg National Military Park in Mississippi, and Shiloh National Military Park in Mississippi and Tennessee.

One final note: Cancellations are no longer available at ranger contact stations. Budget cuts have pared skilled staff to the bone in most national parks, and even when there is enough staff, rangers often leave the stations to perform field duties. If you're a veteran collector, you may have heard that Passport cancellations were available at Rocky Springs Contact Station, Clinton Visitor Center, the Mississippi Craft Center, Kosciusko Information Center, French Camp contact station, and the Jeff Busby Gas Station at points along the Natchez Trace. Ernie Price, interpretive specialist for the Natchez Trace Parkway, reported a streamlining effort in summer 2007 to bring the Parkway's Passport program participation under control, drastically reducing the number of cancellations available along the Parkway. Many old cancellations were discarded in this effort.

Don't miss this! The stamping stops on the parkway only represent a few of the numerous opportunities to discover history, wander in the wilderness, and take part in some Southern hospitality. Keep an eye out for inviting places to pause and admire or explore, as bubbling creeks, shady forests, Indian mounds, nineteenth-century homesteads, and pioneer burial grounds seem to be around every bend.

The Mount Locust Inn, for example, is an old pioneer home, constructed in 1779 and restored to its 1810 appearance, the same year that traffic on the Old Trace reached its peak. It became an overnight stopping place for travelers on the Natchez Trace, using slave labor to serve the people who rested here.

Exhibits tell the inn's story while describing a slave's life in Mount Locust.

In Alabama, George Colbert ran a stand and ferry service at Colbert Ferry in the early 1800s, providing passage across the Tennessee River. There's a story—most likely apocryphal, or at least exaggerated—that Colbert had the audacity to charge U.S. General Andrew Jackson a whopping $75,000 to ferry the general's troops across the river during wartime—a fair bit of change for a boat ride, even by twenty-first century standards! Today this comparatively peaceful spot offers a picnic area with restrooms, swimming, fishing, and a boat launch.

Hours: Natchez Visitor Center/Convention and Visitors Bureau in Mississippi is open Monday to Saturday from 8:30 A.M. to 5:00 P.M., and Sunday from 9:00 A.M. to 4:00 P.M. It is closed on federal holidays.

Mount Locust Information Center in Mississippi is open daily, February to November, from 8:30 A.M. to 5:00 P.M. It is closed in December and January.

Natchez Trace Parkway Visitor Center in Mississippi is open daily year-round, from 8:00 A.M. to 5:00 P.M. It is closed Christmas.

Colbert Ferry Information Center in Alabama is open from 8:00 A.M. to 5:00 P.M. during the summer, but the schedule is change-able. Call the Natchez Trace Parkway Visitor Center in Tupelo for the most up-to-date information.

Fees: There are no fees for use of the parkway, and no admission is charged at any of the cancellation stamp locations.

How to get there: The trace begins in Natchez and continues as a single, northeasterly route to southern Nashville. Addresses and directions to specific stamping sites are provided in the Stamping Locations section.

Stamping Locations and What the Cancellations Say

The cancellations are listed in the order in which you will find them on the parkway, beginning in Natchez at mile 0.

Natchez Visitor Center/Convention and Visitors Bureau
640 South Canal Street, Natchez
(601) 442–7049 or (800) 647–6724
A portion of the building serves as the visitor center for Natchez Historical Park.

☐ Natchez Trace Parkway/AL, MS, TN Ⓓ

☐ Natchez National Historical Park/Melrose Ⓓ

☐ Natchez National Historical Park/William Johnson House Ⓓ

Mount Locust Information Center
Mile 15/16
(601) 445–4211

☐ Natchez Trace Parkway/AL, MS, TN Ⓓ

Natchez Trace Parkway Tupelo Visitor Center
Mile 266, Tupelo
(800) 305–7417

☐ NATCHEZ TRACE PARKWAY/NATIONAL SCENIC TRAIL Ⓓ

☐ Natchez Trace Parkway/Tupelo National Battlefield Ⓤ

☐ Natchez Trace Parkway/AL, MS, TN Ⓓ

☐ Brices Cross Roads Nat'l Battlefield Site/Tupelo, MS Ⓤ
This stamping site is located close to Brices Cross Roads and Tupelo National Battlefields.

Colbert Ferry Information Center
Mile 327.3
(256) 359–6372
Near Colbert Ferry, U.S. Highway 72 forms a major intersection at the parkway's mile marker 320.

☐ NATCHEZ TRACE PARKWAY/NATIONAL SCENIC TRAIL Ⓓ

☐ Natchez Trace Parkway/AL, MS, TN Ⓓ

Headquarters in Blacksburg, South Carolina
(864) 936–3477
www.nps.gov/ovvi
Eastern time zone

Number of cancellations: Five for the trail, plus three cancellations for other national parks

Difficulty: Challenging

About this site: In 1780, patriot militiamen on this route from Virginia through eastern Tennessee, North Carolina, and South Carolina to the battle site at Kings Mountain in South Carolina. These historic roads and trails allowed the militia to track down and defeat an army of loyalists commanded by Major Patrick Ferguson. Visitors can follow the route of the patriots who made the two-week, 330-mile journey to Kings Mountain for the decisive battle that signaled the end of British might in America.

To date, 57 miles of the 330-mile corridor are certified sections of the Overmountain Victory Trail, while the rest are in development. There's also a Commemorative Motor Route that uses state highways. Pick up a map at any of the cancellation sites.

Stamping tips: None of these cancellations are difficult to obtain, as the cancellation sites are all open year-round, but you will travel through three states to collect all five of the unique cancellations. Plan at least three days to do this, as you will want to spend time at each of the stamping sites and in the surrounding communities to understand the magnitude of the troops' accomplishment—traveling hundreds of miles over mountainous terrain, and then soundly defeating the enemy just hours after arriving at Kings Mountain.

Don't miss this! About 7 miles of the Overmountain Victory Trail pass through land managed by W. Kerr Scott Dam and Reservoir, providing an opportunity to hike or mountain bike along the route used by the patriots. Look for the trail logo signs—an Overmountain soldier in profile on a brown and white background. The Overmountain Victory Trail links to two other trails as it passes through the reservoir area: the Dark Mountain Trail, well known for its mountain biking quality, and the Yadkin River Greenway.

Both meet up with the Overmountain at Fish Creek bridge in the park.

Sycamore Shoals preserves part of the first European settlement area west of the Blue Ridge Mountains, where in 1772 settlers established a society hailed as the first in America to use majority vote as a basis for its government. Leaders of the Overmountain patriot march assembled about a thousand men here on September 25, 1780 to begin the trek east. A reproduced Fort Watauga stands on the site today.

Hours: The **Overmountain Victory Trail** Commemorative Motor Route is open twenty-four hours a day, seven days a week.

The **W. Kerr Scott Reservoir Visitor Assistance Center** is open year-round, Monday to Friday from 7:30 A.M. to 5:00 P.M., and Saturday and Sunday from 8:00 A.M. to 4:00 P.M.

The **Museum of North Carolina Minerals** is open daily year-round, from 9:00 A.M. to 5:00 P.M.

Sycamore Shoals State Historic Area Visitor Center is open daily year-round, Monday through Saturday from 8 A.M. to 4:30 P.M., and Sunday from 1:00 to 4:30 P.M.

Cowpens National Battlefield Visitor Center is open daily year-round, from 9:00 A.M. to 5:00 P.M. The auto loop road and picnic area close at 4:30 P.M. It is closed Thanksgiving, Christmas, and New Year's Day.

Kings Mountain National Military Park is open daily year-round, from 9:00 A.M. to 5:00 P.M. It is closed Thanksgiving, Christmas, and New Year's Day.

Fees: Admission to the trail is free.

How to get there: The Commemorative Motor Route begins in Abingdon, Virginia, and ends at Kings Mountain National Military Park in South Carolina. A map with complete directions for traveling the entire route by car is available at cancellation stamping sites. Directions to the stamping sites are provided in the Stamping Locations section.

Stamping Locations and What the Cancellations Say
Sycamore Shoals State Historic Area Visitor Center
1651 West Elk Avenue, Elizabethton, Tennessee
(423) 543–5808
From Knoxville, take Interstate 81 east to Interstate 26. Turn south on I–26, and continue to Johnson City at exit 24. From the

exit, take U.S. Highway 321/Tennessee 91 east for 6 miles to Elizabethton. The park is on the left as you approach Elizabethton.

☐ Overmountain Victory Nat'l Historic Trail/TENNESSEE ⓤ

W. Kerr Scott Dam and Reservoir visitor center
499 Reservoir Road, Wilkesboro, North Carolina
(336) 921–3390
From U.S. Highway 421 in northwestern North Carolina, take exit 286B. Turn onto North Carolina 268 west, go 3 miles, and turn right onto Reservoir Road at the W. KERR SCOTT DAM AND RESERVOIR sign. Go 0.25 mile, and turn left beside Shady Grove Baptist Church.

☐ Overmountain Victory Trail/W. Kerr Scott Dam & Reservoir ⓤ

Museum of North Carolina Minerals
Blue Ridge Parkway, mile 331.0 in North Carolina
(828) 765–2761

☐ Overmountain Victory Trail/Blue Ridge Parkway ⓤ

☐ Blue Ridge Parkway/Museum of N.C. Minerals ⓤ

Cowpens National Battlefield Visitor Center
Chesnee, South Carolina
(864) 461–2828
From Interstate 85 north of Spartanburg, take exit 83. Turn left on South Carolina 110. Drive 8 miles. Turn right on South Carolina 11. The park entrance is about 0.5 mile on the right.

From I–85 southbound, take exit 92 at Gaffney, and head west toward Chesnee on SC 11. The park is about 10 miles down the road on the left.

☐ Overmountain Victory Trail/Cowpens NB ⓤ

☐ Cowpens National Battlefield/Chesnee, SC ⓤ

Kings Mountain National Military Park Visitor Center
Blacksburg, South Carolina
2625 Park Road
(864) 936–7921
From Greenville, take I–85 north to North Carolina exit 2. From Charlotte, North Carolina, travel south on I–85 to exit 2. Continue southeast on South Carolina 216 to the park at 2625 Park Road.

☐ Overmountain Victory Nat'l Hist. Trail/South Carolina **①**

☐ Kings Mountain Nat'l Military Park/Blacksburg, SC **①**

72 Trail of Tears National Historic Trail

Headquarters in Santa Fe, New Mexico
(505) 988–6888
www.nps.gov/trte
Eastern time zone

Number of cancellations: Twenty-two for the trail; nine for other national park sites. More cancellations are available in Illinois, Arkansas, Missouri, and Oklahoma.

Difficulty: Challenging

About this site: In 1838, by order of the United States government, all Indians east of the Mississippi River were forced to surrender their homes and towns to white Americans and move to the designated Indian Territory in Oklahoma. To facilitate this evacuation, the U.S. Army herded some 16,000 Cherokee Indians and as many as 80,000 people of the Choctaw, Creek, Chickasaw, and Seminole tribes into stockades in Alabama, Georgia, Tennessee, and North Carolina, and then into internment camps in Tennessee, where they awaited final relocation.

The subsequent march west to Oklahoma virtually destroyed the Cherokees. Hundreds of people died en route to the Indian Territory, while thousands more died later as a result of the adverse conditions they endured on the way. The Trail of Tears commemorates the Cherokee relocation experience, reminding us that more than 100,000 Indians suffered evacuation and banishment from their native lands.

Stamping tips: The trail passes through North Carolina, Tennessee, Kentucky, Illinois, Georgia, Alabama, Arkansas, Missouri and Oklahoma. Cancellations are available in all of these states, as well as at the National Trails headquarters office in New Mexico.

You'll find Passport cancellations in five states in the Southeast region, and while many of these cancellations are duplicates, the task of collecting all the varieties will take you several days. Choose your travel days carefully, as many of the sites are privately run on limited funds and do not keep daily, year-round hours.

In North Carolina, the Museum of the Cherokee Indian is open daily, but the Cherokee County Historical Museum and Junaluska Museum are not open on Sunday, and the Junaluska Museum closes on Saturday in winter.

A simple rule to follow for Trail of Tears sites in Georgia: Your best bet is to travel Wednesday through Saturday. All of these sites are closed on Monday except for Monday holidays, when two of them open for the holiday and close on Tuesday. Each site is otherwise open year-round.

You have many cancellation collecting choices for the Trail of Tears in Tennessee, including the opportunity to pick up one of the trail's Georgia cancellations. If you're not collecting duplicate cancellations, you will find all three variations of the Trail of Tears cancellations—Tennessee, Georgia, and the list of state abbreviations—at Shiloh, Stones River, and Great Smoky Mountains national park sites. These parks are open daily year-round.

Don't miss this! A brand-new exhibit at the Museum of the Cherokee Indian in North Carolina takes visitors back 12,000 years to understand the Paleo-Indians, ancestors of the Cherokee and the earliest human beings to walk these lands. At the Cherokee County Historical Museum in Murphy, collector Arthur Palmer's extensive collection of Cherokee artifacts—more than 2,000 items he discovered in the area—found a home after Palmer's death in 1972.

The Chieftains Museum in Georgia preserves the story of Major Ridge, a Cherokee leader who worked to promote adoption of the Euro-American culture into Cherokee life, embracing democracy and education. This was the plantation home he gave up when he relocated to Okalahoma in 1837.

New Echota was the capital of the Cherokee Nation, and much of the nation's history remains here on this site. As you tour the reconstructed buildings, you will see many nineteenth-century artifacts of Cherokee life—a crossing of two disparate cultures to blend elements of both in a new set of laws, traditions, and beliefs.

The Trail of Tears Commemorative Park and Heritage Center in Kentucky is one of the few documented sites at which Cherokees camped during their forced march to Oklahoma. Chief Whitepath and Fly Smith, two Cherokee chiefs who died during the evacuation, are buried here and recognized with bronze statues.

In Vonore, Tennessee, the Sequoyah Birthplace Museum tells the amazing story of the man who created the writing system for the Cherokee language, developing eighty-five symbols and bringing literacy to the Cherokee people. Nearby Red Clay State Park was the last bastion of Cherokee government in the period just before the march to Oklahoma began. You'll see a reconstructed National Council House, as well as log buildings that represent the Cherokee homestead and farmland that existed on the site until 1838.

Hours and fees: The **Museum of the Cherokee Indian** is open daily from 9:00 A.M. to 5:00 P.M. It is closed on New Year's Day, Thanksgiving, and Christmas. Admission is $9.00 for adults, $6.00 for children six to thirteen, and free for children five and under.

The **Cherokee County Historical Museum** is open from Memorial Day to Labor Day, Monday through Friday from 9:00 A.M. to 5:00 P.M., and Saturday from 9:00 A.M. to 3:00 P.M. From Labor Day to Memorial Day, the museum is open Monday through Friday from 9:00 A.M. to 5:00 P.M. It is closed on holidays. Admission is $3.00 for adults and $1.00 for children.

Junaluska Memorial and Museum is open from April to August, Monday through Saturday, from 7:45 A.M. to 4:30 P.M. From September through March, the museum is open Monday to Friday from 7:45 A.M. to 4:30 P.M. Free admission.

Chief Vann House Historic Site is open Tuesday to Saturday from 9:00 A.M. to 5:00 P.M., and Sunday from 2:00 P.M. to 5:30 P.M. It is closed on Monday unless that day is a holiday; it is closed Tuesday if open on a Monday holiday. Closed on New Year's Day, Thanksgiving, and Christmas. Admission is $4.00 for adults, $2.50 for children eighteen and under, and $3.50 for seniors sixty-five and older.

Chieftains Museum/Major Ridge Home is open Tuesday through Friday from 9:00 A.M. to 3:00 P.M., and Saturday from 10:00 A.M. to 4:00 P.M. It is closed on Sunday, Monday, and holidays. Free admission.

New Echota Historic Site/Cherokee Capital is open Tuesday through Saturday from 9:00 A.M. to 5:00 P.M., and Sunday from 2:00 to 5:30 P.M. It is closed on Monday unless that day is a holiday; it is closed on Tuesday if open on a Monday holiday. It is closed on New Year's Day, Thanksgiving, and Christmas. Admission is $4.00 for adults, $2.50 for children eighteen and under.

The **Trail of Tears Commemorative Park** in Kentucky is open daily. It is closed from 10:00 P.M. to sunrise on weekdays, and 11:00 P.M. to sunrise on Saturday and Sunday. When the heritage center at the park is open, its season is April to October, Monday to Saturday, from 10:00 A.M. to 4:00 P.M. From November to March, it is open Tuesday to Saturday from 10:00 A.M. to 2:00 P.M. It is closed on Sunday and holidays. Admission to this park is free.

The **Little River Canyon National Preserve** superintendent's office is open Monday to Friday from 8:00 A.M. to 4:30 P.M., and Saturday from 10:00 A.M. to 2:00 P.M. It is closed on all major holidays. Free admission.

Russell Cave National Monument is open daily year-round, from 8:00 A.M. to 4:30 P.M. It is closed Thanksgiving, Christmas, and New Year's Day. Free admission.

Audubon Acres is open Monday through Saturday from 9:00 A.M. to 5:00 P.M., and Sunday 1:00 to 5:00 P.M. The grounds are open daily until dusk. The site is closed on New Year's Day, Memorial Day, July 4, Labor Day, Thanksgiving, and Christmas. There is no admission fee, but a donation is requested.

Chattanooga Regional History Museum is open Memorial Day to Labor Day, Monday to Friday from 10:00 A.M. to 4:30 P.M., and Saturday and Sunday from 11:00 A.M. to 4:30 P.M. From Labor Day to Memorial Day, the museum is open Monday to Friday from 10:00 A.M. to 4:30 P.M., and Saturday and Sunday from 11:00 A.M. to 4:00 P.M. It is closed on New Year's Day, Thanksgiving, and Christmas. Admission is $4.00 for adults, $3.50 for senior citizens, $3.00 for children five to eighteen, and free for children four and under.

Great Smoky Mountains National Park, Sugarlands Visitor Center is open daily year-round, from 8:00 A.M. to 6:00 P.M. The center has extended hours June to August, from 8:00 A.M. to 7:00 P.M. Admission is free.

Hermitage Mansion is open daily from 9:00 A.M. to 5:00 P.M. It is closed Thanksgiving, Christmas, and the third week in January. Admission for adults is $12.00; seniors and students (thirteen to eighteen) are $11.00, and children (six to twelve) are $6.00. Children five and under are free.

Lookout Mountain Battlefield Visitor Center is open daily from 8:30 A.M. to 5:00 P.M. It is closed Christmas. Admission is $3.00 for adults and children sixteen and older; free for children under sixteen.

Red Clay State Park Visitor Center is open Sunday from 1:00 to 4:30 P.M., and Wednesday through Saturday from 8:00 A.M. to 4:30 P.M. The visitor center is closed on Monday and Tuesday, and December 22 through January 1. Admission is free, but there are fees for the use of facilities and rentals.

Sequoyah Birthplace Museum is open Monday through Saturday from 9:00 A.M. to 5:00 P.M., and Sunday from noon to 5:00 P.M. It is closed on New Year's Day, Thanksgiving, and Christmas. Admission is $3.00 for adults, $2.50 for seniors, and $1.50 for children six to twelve. Admission is free for children five and under.

Shiloh National Military Park is open daily year-round, from 8:00 A.M. to 5:00 P.M. It is closed Christmas. Admission is $5.00 per vehicle, good for seven days. Individuals on foot, bicycle, or motorcycle are admitted for $3.00, good for seven days.

Stones River National Battlefield is open daily from 8:00 A.M. to 5:00 P.M. It is closed Christmas. Admission is free.

Tennessee River Museum is open daily, Monday through Saturday from 9:00 A.M. to 5:00 P.M., and Sunday from 1:00 to 5:00 P.M. It is closed Thanksgiving and Christmas. Admission is $2.00 for adults and free for children eighteen and under. Patrons are admitted free with orange admission tickets from Shiloh National Military Park.

How to get there: Directions to each site are provided in the Stamping Locations section.

Stamping Locations and What the Cancellations Say

Cancellation stamp sites are listed alphabetically by state. Time zones are included.

Little River Canyon National Preserve

2141 Gault Avenue North, Fort Payne, Alabama
(256) 845–9605
Central time zone
From Atlanta, Georgia, take Interstate 75 north to exit 290. Turn left after exiting onto Georgia 20. Follow the road 4 miles. Turn

left onto U.S. Highway 411. Bear right onto Joe Frank Harris Parkway Southeast, and continue for 3 miles. Take the ramp onto US 411 south to Rome, Georgia. Take the U.S. Highway 27 north ramp, and continue on this road for 3 miles. Pick up GA 20 going west, and stay on GA 20 as it turns into Alabama 9. Follow AL 9 for 6 or 7 miles to its intersection with Alabama 35 toward Fort Payne.

☐ Trail of Tears NHT/Alabama ⓤ
  The cancellation is in the superintendent's office.

☐ Little River Canyon National Preserve/Ft. Payne, AL ⓓ

Russell Cave National Monument
Gilbert H. Grosvenor Visitor Center
Bridgeport, Alabama
From U.S. Highway 72, follow County Road 75 north 1 mile to County Road 98. Follow CR 98 north 4 miles to the park entrance at 3729 CR 98.

☐ Trail of Tears NHT/Alabama ⓓ

☐ Russell Cave National Monument/Bridgeport, AL 35740 ⓤ

☐ Little River Canyon Nat'l Preserve/Fort Payne, AL ⓓ

Chieftains Museum/Major Ridge Home
501 Riverside Parkway Northeast, Rome, Georgia
(706) 291–9494
Eastern time zone
Located between the Georgia 53 spur and U.S. Highway 27 in Rome

☐ Trail of Tears National Historic Trail/Georgia ⓓ

Chief Vann House Historic Site
82 Georgia Highway 225 North, Chatsworth, Georgia
(706) 695–2598
Eastern time zone
Located at the intersection of Georgia 225 and Georgia 52A, on the outskirts of Chatsworth

☐ Trail of Tears National Historic Trail/Georgia ⓓ

New Echota Historic Site/Cherokee Capital
1211 Chatsworth Highway Northeast, Calhoun, Georgia
(706) 624–1321
Eastern time zone
Located on Georgia 225 about 0.5 mile east of Interstate 75 in
Gordon County

☐ Trail of Tears National Historic Trail/Georgia **ⓓ**

Tennessee River Museum
507 Main Street, Savannah, Georgia
(800) 552–3866
Central time zone
Main Street is U.S. Highway 64 in the town of Savannah.

☐ Trail of Tears National Historic Trail/NC, GA, TN, KY, AL, IL,
   MO, OK, AR **ⓓ**

☐ Trail of Tears National Historic Trail/Tennessee **ⓓ**

Trail of Tears Commemorative Park and Heritage Center
Hopkinsville, Kentucky
(270) 886–8033
Central time zone
The Trail of Tears stamping site is at U.S. Highway 41 and Skyline
Drive in Hopkinsville. From Nashville, Tennessee, take Interstate
24 north to the junction with US 41 at exit 86. Continue north on
US 41 to Hopkinsville, where it becomes US Alternate 41. Take
US Alternate 41 into town to the intersection with Skyline Drive.

☐ Trail of Tears National Historic Trail/NC, GA, TN, KY, AL, IL,
   MO, OK **ⓓ**

☐ Trail of Tears National Historic Trail/Kentucky **ⓤ**

Cherokee Country Historical Museum
87 Peachtree Street, Murphy, North Carolina
(828) 837–6792
Eastern time zone
From Cherokee, take U.S. Highway 19 south to Hyatt Creek
Road (about 5 miles). Turn left, and merge onto U.S. Highway 74
west. Drive about 50 miles to Murphy. Once in town, stay on US
74 to Peachtree Street, and turn right on Peachtree. The museum

is about half a mile down the street. It is located in the two-story, stone Carnegie Library Building.

☐ Trail of Tears National Historic Trail/North Carolina ⒟

Junaluska Memorial and Museum

Junaluska Drive/U.S. Highway 129, Robbinsville, North Carolina
(828) 479–4727
Eastern time zone
From Cherokee, take US 19 to US 129. Turn right on US 129, and continue to Robbinsville, at the junction with North Carolina 143. The memorial is just beyond this junction.

☐ Trail of Tears National Historic Trail/North Carolina ⒟

Museum of the Cherokee Indian

589 Tsali Boulevard, Cherokee, North Carolina
(828) 497–3481
Eastern time zone
From the east, take Interstate 40 west to exit 27 for U.S. Highway 74. Travel west on US 74 to exit 74 (for Cherokee/Great Smoky Mountains National Park). Bear right on exit 74, and proceed about 5 miles north on US 441 to the third traffic light. Turn right, and go about 0.5 mile to the next traffic light. Turn left, and continue on US 441 north. Proceed 0.6 mile to the next traffic light (the intersection of US 441 and Tsali Boulevard). Turn left. The museum is on the left.

☐ Trail of Tears National Historic Trail/North Carolina ⒟
The cancellation is in the box office.

Audubon Acres

900 North Sanctuary Road, Chattanooga, Tennessee
(423) 892–1499
Eastern time zone
From Interstate 75, take exit 3A to East Brainerd Road–East. At the second traffic light, turn right onto Gunbarrel Road. Follow Gunbarrel Road as it becomes North Sanctuary Road. It reaches the dead end at Audubon Acres in about 2 miles.

☐ Trail of Tears National Historic Trail/Tennessee ⒟

Chattanooga Regional History Museum

400 Chestnut Street, Chattanooga, Tennessee

(423) 423–3247

Eastern time zone

Located at the corner of Fourth and Chestnut Streets in Chattanooga. From Interstate 24, take U.S. Highway 27N to exit 1C (Fourth Street).

☐ Trail of Tears National Historic Trail/Tennessee **Ⓓ**

Great Smoky Mountains National Park, Sugarlands Visitor Center desk

Gatlinburg, Tennessee

(865) 436–1291

Eastern time zone

Located inside the park, 2 miles south of Gatlinburg on U.S. Highway 441

☐ Trail of Tears National Historic Trail/Tennessee **Ⓓ**

☐ Great Smoky Mountains National Park/Sugarland VC/ Tennessee **Ⓤ**

Hermitage Mansion, Home of Andrew Jackson

4580 Rachel's Lane, Nashville, Tennessee

(615) 889–2941 ext. 220

Central time zone

Located 12 miles east of downtown Nashville. The site is accessible from Interstate 40, exit 221A (the Hermitage exit). From Interstate 65 northbound, the Hermitage is accessible from exit 92 for Old Hickory Boulevard South.

☐ Trail of Tears National Historic Trail/Tennessee **Ⓓ**

Lookout Mountain Battlefield Visitor Center

Chickamauga and Chattanooga National Battlefield Park, Tennessee

(423) 821–7786

Eastern time zone

From Nashville, take Interstate 24 south to exit 174, and then go south on US 41. Take Tennessee 148 to the top of Lookout Mountain, and go right on East Brow Road. Point Park and the visitor center are at the end of East Brow Road.

☐ Trail of Tears National Historic Trail/Georgia **Ⓓ**

☐ ChCh NMP Lookout Mtn. National Battlefield/
Lookout Mtn, TN **Ⓤ**

Red Clay State Park
1140 Red Clay Park Road, Cleveland, Tennessee
(423) 478–0339
Eastern time zone
The park is located in Bradley County, along the Tennessee-
Georgia state line about 17 miles southeast of Chattanooga.
From Chattanooga, take Interstate 75 south to exit 3-A (East
Brainerd Road). Turn to the east on Brainerd, and drive 8 miles to
London Lane. Continue on London Lane for just more than 2
miles, where it becomes Keith Road. Continue for half a mile on
Keith Road to Mount Vernon Road, and turn left. Drive 4 miles to
Old Apison Road, and continue for 7 miles to Red Clay Park
Road. Turn left; the park is 1.5 miles down the road.

☐ Trail of Tears National Historic Trail/NC, GA, TN, KY, AL, IL,
MO, OK, AR **Ⓓ**

☐ Trail of Tears National Historic Trail/Tennessee **Ⓓ**

Sequoyah Birthplace Museum
576 Tennessee 360, Vonore, Tennessee
(423) 884–6246
Eastern time zone
From Nashville, take Interstate 40 east to Interstate 75 southbound. Exit I–75 onto Tennessee 72 eastbound, and follow TN 72
to Vonore. Turn left on US 411 northbound and follow the highway to a right turn onto Tennessee 360 at a traffic light. Continue
to the museum.

☐ Trail of Tears National Historic Trail/Tennessee **Ⓓ**

Shiloh National Military Park bookstore
1055 Pittsburg Landing Road, Shiloh, Tennessee
(731) 689–5696
Central time zone
From Interstate 40 west of Nashville, exit at Lexington, and take
Tennessee 22 south to Shiloh. From Memphis, take Tennessee 57
east to TN 22, and head north to Shiloh.

☐ Trail of Tears National Historic Trail/NC, GA, TN, KY, IL, MO, OK, AR **Ⓓ**

☐ Shiloh NMP/Shiloh, TN **Ⓤ**

Stones River National Battlefield Visitor Center

3501 Old Nashville Highway, Murfreesboro, Tennessee
(615) 478–1035
Central time zone
From Interstate 24 south of Nashville, take exit 78B. Follow Tennessee 96 to its intersection with U.S. Highways 41/70. Turn left, and take US 41/70 north to Thompson Lane. Turn left on Thompson Lane. Exit to Old Nashville Highway, and follow the signs to the battlefield.

☐ Trail of Tears National Historic Trail/Tennessee **Ⓓ**

☐ Stones River National Battlefield/Murfreesboro, TN **Ⓤ**

☐ Stones River NB/Underground RR Freedom Network **Ⓤ**

☐ Tennessee Civil War NHA/Murfreesboro, TN **Ⓓ**

About the Author

Randi Minetor has visited more than 200 national parks, and has written several books for FalconGuides, including the *Passport To Your National Parks® Companion Guides* series and two *National Park Pocket Guides*. Randi served as a consultant and writer for Eastern National's *Passport Explorer,* the big brother to the best-selling *Passport To Your National Parks®* book. Her groundbreaking book *Breadwinner Wives and the Men They Marry* (New Horizon Press, 2002) continues to receive national media attention, and her articles have appeared in dozens of trade magazines on subjects ranging from municipal water system management to technical theater. She and her husband, Nic, live in Rochester, New York.